insight text guide

Timothy Roberts

# Things We Didn't See Coming

Steven Amsterdam

First published in 2010. Reprinted 2012, 2017, 2019, 2021, 2023.

Insight Publications Pty Ltd
3/350 Charman Road
Cheltenham VIC 3192
Australia
Tel: +61 3 8571 4950
Fax: +61 3 8571 0257
Email: books@insightpublications.com.au

**www.insightpublications.com.au**



National Library of Australia Cataloguing-in-Publication entry:
Roberts, Timothy, 1979-
Steven Amsterdam's things we didn't see coming /
Timothy Roberts.
9781921411793 (pbk.)
Insight text guide.
For secondary school age.
Amsterdam, Steven; Things we didn't see coming.
823.8

Other ISBNs:
9781925316612 (digital)
9781925316629 (bundle: print + digital)

Cover design: The Modern Art Production Group

Printed by Markono Print Media Pte Ltd

# contents

# CHARACTER MAP

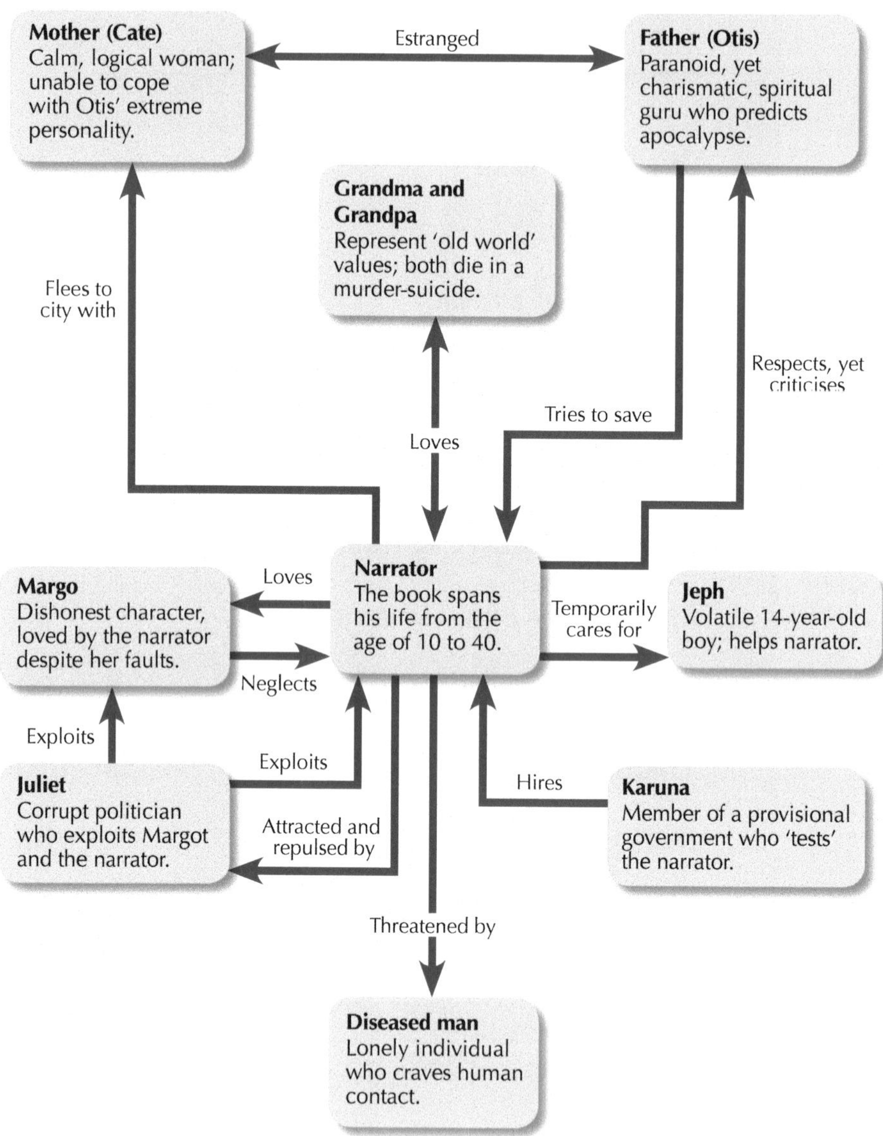

# OVERVIEW

## About the author

Steven Amsterdam lives in Melbourne, having grown up in New York City. He has worked in many occupations, including as a pastry chef, a book designer and a psychiatric and palliative care nurse at Melbourne's The Alfred hospital. Although he has published several short stories, *Things We Didn't See Coming* is Amsterdam's first extended work of fiction. The book – a series of stories – met with remarkable success in Australia, winning *The Age* Book of the Year award in 2009, among several others.

Clearly, some of his prior experiences have helped him in writing the book, especially its palliative care-themed final chapter: 'My main interests in nursing have been palliative care and psychiatry, and they both involve patients who tend to be patients for a long period of time, rather than someone who comes in, gets a heart valve replacement and goes on home' (Rabelais 2009). Amsterdam's vivid depiction of the drawn-out pain of the terminally ill in *Cakewalk* and *Best Medicine* demonstrate his ability to dramatise prolonged suffering.

One of Amsterdam's notable personal characteristics is his acute sensitivity to current threats, both real and imagined. For him, a threat does not actually have to be real for it to be frightening. He admits, for example, that 'to "celebrate" Y2K, my ex and I packed the car and rented a house in the country. He was calm, I was the nervous one' (Cunningham 2010). In another interview, he confesses, 'I have been known to worry about many things, including Y2K, pandemic, climate change, war. You name it' (Meyer 2010). Amsterdam is clearly not ashamed of being labelled an acute worrier. The first story, *What We Know Now*, could therefore be seen as a small joke at Amsterdam's own expense: perhaps the father's character, with his extreme reaction to events, contains elements of Amsterdam's own personality.

Although Amsterdam is aware of our planet's real and urgent problems, environmental collapse is not the primary focus of *Things We Didn't See Coming*. He acknowledges that his book is largely a 'thought experiment' in which environmental events take second place to characters' reactions. His interests do not lie in technology itself, but rather in the often surprising ways in which people react to sudden and jarring environmental change. In his own words, 'the book isn't about climate change and plague. It's about the little things that will always be closer to our concerns' (Meyer 2010).

## Synopsis

The book is set amidst a series of catastrophic events that take place in the early to mid 21st century – from the end of 1999 to about 2030 – and describes a minutely detailed and terrifyingly plausible alternative future in which the planet is no longer capable of adequately supporting human life.

The stories are loosely structured around a series of disasters, both natural and man-made. These stories, written in the first person, are linked by a nameless narrator whose circumstances are constantly shifting.

- As a boy of 10, the narrator is prepared by his father to flee from the potentially devastating effects of the Y2K bug. (After Y2K passes, he goes to live with his mother in the city.)
- At 17, as a teenager living with his grandparents, he leaves the city for the country on an ill-fated trip, which results in both his grandparents' deaths.
- In his early 20s, he takes on a job evacuating flooded properties for the government, during which an attempt is made on his life.
- In his mid 20s, he lives in a city apartment with his girlfriend Margo, subsequently moving to a tent in the desert when plague hits.
- In his late 20s, he becomes separated from Margo. They are reunited in a refugee camp-type environment, where he works as a verification officer. They manage to escape together.
- In his early 30s, he and Margo become the servants of a charismatic and corrupt political leader, Juliet. Soon after, he leaves Margo for good.
- In his mid 30s, living in a small rural community, he is made the guardian of a troubled 14-year-old boy named Jeph. Feeling constrained by this environment, he soon escapes, leaving Jeph to fend for himself.

- In his late 30s, he is 'elected' to a provisional government, established to restore order after the wave of disasters in previous chapters.
- Finally, aged about 40, stricken with skin cancer, he reunites with his estranged father to die – or perhaps to be cured.

## Character list

**The protagonist:** The male narrator is around 10 when the book begins, and around 40 when it finishes. We see the entire world through his eyes.

Although he is not a particularly charismatic character, the protagonist possesses an integrity that many around him lack. Most of the time, he does what he can to help others – a trait that makes him better than many of the people around him.

**The father (Otis):** A rather ambiguous character, Otis is the 'prophet' of the story. He predicts the Y2K disaster, and tries in vain to prepare his family for the worst. Then, during a long period apart from his son, he establishes himself as an exile from the rest of society. The two finally reunite in the final story, when the narrator is terminally ill.

**The mother (Cate):** Although the narrator's mother is only featured in the first story, she is shown to be a loving mother who does not fully understand the significance of what is happening. The narrator lives with her for some years after the first story takes place, before she moves to a desert town and trains to be a servant (p.113). She dies sometime between *Uses for Vinegar* and *The Forest for the Trees*.

**The Grandparents:** The protagonist's grandfather and grandmother represent old-fashioned values, which are sorely lacking in the rest of the novel. Although they are fundamentally decent people, the couple is utterly unequipped to cope with the challenges of the harsh new world they find themselves in. After a delusional flirtation with freedom in *The Theft That Got Me Here*, the grandfather tragically chooses to end both of their lives.

**Liz and Jenna:** The protagonist finds Liz and Jenna, a mother and daughter, in an old farmhouse, and unsuccessfully attempts to evacuate them. Although they are filthy and starving, they demonstrate a fierce protective instinct toward each other: the narrator's attempt to convince the daughter to leave with him is unsuccessful. Eventually, they make an attempt on his life.

**Margo:** The protagonist's lover and main source of inspiration for much of the narrative, Margo is presented as an unworthy object of his love. Unlike the narrator, she is self-centred and pleasure-seeking. The two separate after Margo befriends Juliet.

**Juliet:** A rich and unscrupulous politician, Juliet is blatantly uninterested in the welfare of her supporters. She befriends the narrator and Margo, turning them into pawns in her hedonistic game.

**Jeph:** A teenage boy, whom the narrator is assigned to care for. Although Jeph is impolite and arrogant at times, he also shares some of the narrator's positive qualities, such as compassion and loyalty.

**Karuna:** The superficially kind and attractive Karuna is actually a deceptive character who attempts to catch the narrator out in a lie. However, despite the fact that her job as an interviewer for the provisional government requires her to lie and act somewhat abruptly, she is nevertheless relatively appealing.

# BACKGROUND & CONTEXT

Many currents running through Amsterdam's novel are intensely relevant to today's world. Although the setting is unspecified, it seems likely to be in the US. The characters' dialogue sounds American, and certain subtle details – such as the emphasis on freeways and big cars, the Presidential-style politics featured in *The Forest for the Trees*, and the reference to the Amish in *Predisposed* (p.133) – suggest the US, although it is difficult to be certain.

## Environmental disasters

The US, like most industrialised countries, has suffered a long history of man-made environmental disasters. For example, in the 19th century the American buffalo, which originally numbered in the tens of millions, was almost wiped out by hunters. However, accelerated industrialisation during the 20th century caused these disasters to occur on a much larger scale. In *Things We Didn't See Coming,* Amsterdam imagines an unceasing series of modern environmental disasters which, combined, manage to cripple humanity by destroying the resource base of industrial society.

Of course, environmental catastrophes don't just happen in fiction. At the time of writing, for example, the US was experiencing the worst oil spill in its history: the BP oil spill, which began in the Gulf of Mexico in May 2010, rapidly became an environmental catastrophe. Journalist Bob Herbert, a *New York Times* columnist, summed up the national mood of despair:

> No one can say what terrible toll the gusher is taking in the depths of the gulf. And spreading right along with the oil is a pervasive and dismaying sense of helplessness from our leaders in Washington. (Herbert 2010)

This real-life disaster, like those in the book, has caused widespread disillusionment with the US government. Environmental disasters are partially a result of our modern lifestyle, made possible by our uncritical dependence on advanced technology.

Some man-made disasters have had a particularly severe and lasting impact on the planet. For instance, the shocking 1986 disaster in Chernobyl, Ukraine (at that time a part of the Soviet Union), in which a nuclear reactor melted down, contaminated thousands of people and spread radioactive waste across the USSR and Europe.

Natural disasters take their toll, too. In 2004, for example, the Asian Tsunami killed hundreds of thousands of people. In the past few years alone, we have feared Mad Cow Disease, Bird Flu, Swine Flu and SARS, all previously unknown diseases. Usually, modern medicine manages to contain potential epidemics.

However, an inevitable sense of 'disease fatigue' eventually sets in. Sooner or later, people get the sense that the media is 'crying wolf' about environmental threats. Amsterdam's book, then, can be seen as a kind of thought experiment: what if all the warnings were *true*? What if everything we are warned about actually *happened*? His answer is disturbing: our deeply interconnected society may not be able to withstand repeated assaults.

## Apocalyptic fears

Fears of the end of the world have always been with us. The Mayans, for example, a civilisation which existed in Central America from approximately 2000 BC until their eventual collapse in around 900 AD, famously believed that the world would end in the year 2012. In his book *Millennium*, Tom Holland explains how Christians also anticipated the destruction – and subsequent resurrection – of the entire world:

> Rome would fall, and deadly portents afflict mankind, and Satan ... escape his prison, until at last, in the final hour of reckoning, Christ would come again, and all the world be judged, and Satan and his followers be condemned to a pit of fire. (Holland 2009)

These fears of worldwide destruction have recurred throughout history. Although the characters in *Things We Didn't See Coming* lack religious belief, many of the visions of destruction sound distinctly religious. However, Amsterdam's world does not seem to hold any definitive hope of a final resurrection. The narrator, while aware of these visions, remains sceptical:

> I'll get that slight nausea that tells me: sure, that's exactly what this is. Jesus will come home and you'll be caught holding a big bag of Eternal Damnation. But I still don't buy it or maybe tonight I'm just not that enticed by the Kingdom of Heaven. (p.91)

Despite the narrator's flippant attitude and his claims to be non-religious, his mind is still deeply affected by this apocalyptic religious imagery.

## The Y2K bug

Y2K was an anti-climactic event that faded into memory quickly. Shortly before the Year 2000, computer experts around the world realised that there was a problem with the way computers calculated dates. To save memory, the inventors of computers in the 1960s gave them an abridged two-digit calendar (e.g. '74' instead of '1974'). This worked well until 1999, but when 2000 loomed, many feared that the world's computers, mistakenly thinking that it was 1900, would soon reset themselves to the year '00'. The father's fears in the first chapter are amusing to those who lived through the Y2K 'scare', because on 1 January 2000 ... nothing happened.

Amsterdam suggests, however, that our Y2K fears had a logical basis. The dangers of being excessively interconnected are foremost in the writer's mind; everything's so tangled up in our society that if one part goes, everything else is bound to follow. According to *Wired* magazine, the fact that 'fewer American kids are growing up to be bona fide computer geeks ... poses a serious security risk for the country' (Drummond 2010). Given that a few well-trained hackers theoretically have the potential to take down the world's telecommunications network, worrying about excessive interconnectedness seems logical.

## Political and social divisions

It is easy to overlook the political conflicts hinted at in the book, but they are definitely there. The society depicted by Amsterdam has become riven with divisions, the most important being the one between city-dwellers and country-dwellers. The novel's urban population has become completely separated from the rural population by the latter's monopoly over resources. These two social groups are basically at war with each other. Country residents starve city residents of resources, locking them into a prison-like urban space that is eternally plagued by starvation, scarcity and unrest.

In some ways, Amsterdam's book can be seen as a comment on the real-life political divisions that have opened up in the US in recent decades. He mentions that observing 'the 2004 election in the US' helped motivate him to write the book (Meyer 2009). Since Barack Obama's 2008 election, the US political landscape has become further polarised. Although Obama was elected in the hope that the two rival sides of politics could overcome their differences and work together, this hasn't happened. As Amsterdam says, 'in America many people are losing their jobs, many people are losing their grip on their dream. The whole healthcare thing is such a nightmare' (Cunningham 2010). The divided world of *Things We Didn't See Coming*, then, can be seen as a reflection of the US today.

While doomsayers have always speculated about the imminent collapse of the US, several people have recently predicted that it may end up like the Roman Empire:

> Hollowed out by arrogance, corruption and a bloated military, the greatest empire the world has ever known fell. Is America doomed to follow in its footsteps? (Kamiya 2007)

Amsterdam seems aware of this mood. The society depicted in the novel has been brought to its knees, with law and order collapsing, and the country split into separate territories. For example, the Senator's effort in *The Forest for the Trees* to 'expand her power to the West, as far as the ocean' (p.103) suggests that separate states no longer exist, and there is no longer a national government. The series of disasters that befall Amsterdam's world can be read as a logical extension of the comparatively mild current problems of the US, or of any other industrialised country.

## Resource wars

The idea that resource shortages cause conflict is not new. In his book *Collapse,* Jared Diamond points out that the Rwandan genocide of 1994, in which 800,000 people were murdered, was triggered by the country's resources being insufficient for its population. He warns:

> Severe problems of overpopulation, environmental impact, and climate change cannot persist indefinitely: sooner or later they are likely to resolve themselves, whether in the manner of Rwanda or in some other manner not of our own devising. (Diamond 2005, p.328)

Amsterdam makes it clear that unequal distribution of resources is the primary cause of conflict in his novel. When essential resources are in extremely short supply, people riot.

In *The Theft That Got Me Here,* wealthy rural dwellers hoard resources from impoverished urban populations. The city-dwelling narrator is resentful when he first sees the countryside's lush pastures, comparing the landscape to the technicolour scenes of *The Wizard of Oz*. He notes, resentfully, 'They'd let us die of thirst in the city' (p.34).

Worse still, rural dwellers are heartless enough to grow *luxury* items at a time of scarcity, including 'tobacco so bright it practically hurts your eyes' (p.34). The boy and his grandparents are continually amazed at the scenes of abundance:

> We're looking down on an aerial plaid of corn and wheat in endless alternation. Fuel, bread, fuel, bread, fuel, bread. In the distance, a reservoir: enough water. (p.37)

A lack of food has made this society starkly divided. Resource shortages have created a kind of 'apartheid' (separated) system: the 'haves' control everything, while the 'have-nots' receive virtually nothing. The narrator even calls violent crime 'part of the food distribution problem' (p.109).

## The Club of Rome: *Limits to Growth* report

In the late 1960s, an organisation was formed to assess the health of the Earth's resources. In 1972 this organisation, dubbed the 'Club of Rome', released an influential report entitled *Limits to Growth*, which concluded:

> Continued growth in the global economy would lead to planetary limits being exceeded some time in the 21st century, most likely resulting in the collapse of the population and economic system, but also that collapse could be avoided with a combination of changes in behaviour, policy, and technology. (Turner 2008, pp.1–2)

The report – attacked by many – sold 12 million copies and was translated into many languages. *Limits to Growth* has recently received renewed attention. Given current environmental threats, the continued relevance of *Limits to Growth* is food for thought. Amsterdam's book is a useful comment on what might happen when we exceed the Earth's resource limits.

## Border protection

One of the major fault lines running through the book is the urge to secure borders and exclude 'foreigners'. Amsterdam has cleverly incorporated this perennial human conflict into his narrative.

In the US, border protection has long been an emotional issue. The largest source of immigrants is Mexico; the border crossings are a source of constant controversy. In 2010, Arizona's attempt to introduce punitive (harsh) immigration laws that would make it a crime to be in the US without documentation triggered massive protests. This issue is always contentious in Australia, too. In the past decade, Australian politicians have stoked similar public fears of refugees.

# GENRE, STRUCTURE & LANGUAGE

## Genre

### The dystopian/utopian novel

*Things We Didn't See Coming* can be seen as an example of a 'dystopian novel': that is, a novel set in a nightmare world. Amsterdam's bleak picture of the future is intended to shed light on present-day problems.

One of the most famous dystopian novels is William Golding's *Lord of the Flies*, which describes a group of schoolchildren marooned on an island without adults. Although the children initially enjoy their new-found liberation, they soon become violent, and are only saved when adults return. *Lord of the Flies* pessimistically suggests that difficult circumstances bring out the very worst in people.

The opposite to the dystopian novel is the utopian novel, which deals with a 'perfect' world. *Robinson Crusoe*, the story of an Englishman marooned on a desert island, is a classic utopian novel. Unlike the children in *Lord of the Flies*, Crusoe transforms his hostile new environment into a hospitable place through his own ingenuity. *Robinson Crusoe* optimistically claims that good people will often prosper in difficult circumstances.

*Things We Didn't See Coming* falls somewhere between these two extremes. Unlike *Robinson Crusoe*, it does not feature an ideal world in which people flourish. However, unlike *Lord of the Flies*, it doesn't feature a world devoid of human goodness: Amsterdam clearly has faith in humans' capacity to triumph over terrible adversity. The scenes in which people act compassionately, even at great risk to themselves, suggest that Amsterdam is quite optimistic about humanity's virtues.

### The epic journey through Hell

The book can be seen as a kind of retelling of the 'apocalyptic epic' for our modern age. The epic is an extended poetic form, often describing an individual's quest through a terrifying, alienating landscape.

One of the most famous epics, *The Divine Comedy,* was written in the 13th century by Italian poet Dante Alighieri. The most famous of its three parts, *Hell (Inferno),* relates the protagonist's journey through the Nine Circles of Hell, each of which houses a different category of sinner. Even if you haven't read the poem, you may be familiar with the famous line written over the Gate of Dante's Hell: 'Abandon All Hope, Ye Who Enter Here.'

Another epic on which Amsterdam's novel draws is Milton's *Paradise Lost,* which tells the story of the angel Lucifer's struggle against God. Although Lucifer is God's favourite, his ambition motivates him to rebel. After being expelled ('falling') from Heaven, Lucifer rouses his rebel army with the words, 'Better to reign in Hell, than serve in Heaven.' This theme of 'falling' from a perfect past features heavily in *Things We Didn't See Coming,* whose narrator sees himself as having 'fallen', like Lucifer, from the innocent state of his childhood.

Good usually triumphs over evil in the epic. In *Things We Didn't See Coming,* though, the ending is less clear-cut: we are not told whether or not the narrator has finally found peace.

### Science fiction and the future

Although Amsterdam has stated that he 'didn't hear the words "science fiction" until very late in the game' (Cunningham 2010), the book shares the science fiction genre's interest in visions of future worlds.

Amsterdam's world obviously lacks glamour and polish compared to more 'futuristic' narratives such as *Star Wars*. Unlike many science fiction writers, he is fully aware of the impossibility of making predictions. In *The Forest for the Trees*, for example, when Margo and the protagonist watch *Robocop* in Juliet's car, the narrator says that 'the futuristic stuff is just plain funny because they got everything so wrong' (p.109). Amsterdam is making a sly comment to the audience here: in an interview, he noted that 'where the narrator ... smirks at the poorly-predicted future, that's my out for everything I get wrong' (Meyer 2010).

Amsterdam's vision of the future is similar to one we might imagine for our own world in many ways, yet it is also very different, a bizarre melange (mixture) of old and new. There are no shiny, super-intelligent machines as might be expected, because 'robotics fizzled' (p.109). By avoiding the temptation to paint the future as we usually imagine it – as a shiny collection of advanced technology – Amsterdam cleverly subverts our expectations.

### The Bildungsroman ('novel of development')

Although the stories are only loosely connected, the saga resembles a Bildungsroman ('novel of development'), a term referring to the story of a child's growth into a man or woman. This genre of novel focuses on vital changes in the protagonist between childhood and adulthood, representing the process of maturity as a gradual loss of innocence and growing acceptance of the world's limitations.

The protagonist of *Things We Didn't See Coming* changes significantly over the course of his life. In the beginning, he has a reverential attitude towards his father, as we might expect of a young boy convinced of his father's trustworthiness. He is grateful for being involved and trusts his father unreservedly, proudly announcing, 'Dad decides that I can be trusted with the mini-fridge next to me' (p.9).

Yet when the narrator returns to his father about three decades later, he is far more bitter and cynical. Although he acknowledges his father's correct predictions, he has clearly ceased to believe in his infallibility: 'so much for sane', he says dismissively (p.166). As an adult, the narrator often seems to view his father as a gifted crackpot, rather than as a saviour. Like all Bildungsroman narratives, *Things We Didn't See Coming* tells a story of the lost illusions of childhood.

## Structure

### The novel versus the short story

At first glance, *Things We Didn't See Coming* seems to be a series of short stories with the narrative taking the form of a series of separate episodes.

However, these short stories are linked by the protagonist's first-person perspective. *Things We Didn't See Coming* can therefore be seen either as a novel or as a series of linked short stories. For clarity's sake, I have referred to *Things We Didn't See Coming* as a 'novel' throughout this text guide.

### Withheld information

One of Amsterdam's most effective methods of creating suspense through structure is his technique of releasing important information to the reader *gradually*. At the beginning of each story, we receive the bare minimum of information. We only learn to make sense of this disorienting situation in light of extra information that is later revealed.

By keeping readers in the dark, Amsterdam maximises the suspense, and thus the reader's engagement with the text, forcing them to piece together the 'clues' in order to find out what is going on. (Amsterdam's technique of beginning the story in the midst of the action is called *in media res*, Latin for 'in the middle of things'.)

Many terms, objects, customs and behaviours described by the narrator seem foreign, unfamiliar or incomprehensible to us at first. For example, in *What We Know Now*, we don't know why the family is taking 'special measures' to escape (p.7) until much later. Until things become clear, we must decipher the father's motivations ourselves. Given limited information, the reader is only able to understand events by carefully observing the sketchy details provided and drawing logical conclusions.

### Flashbacks and chronological structure

Although the stories appear simple, their timeframe is actually quite complex. The action always begins in the present, but it often dips back into the past to reveal further important information. By piecing together the chronological structure, we can deduce that the narrative spans about 30 years of the protagonist's life.

As mentioned earlier, we know that the first story is set on New Years' Eve 1999. The rest of the stories can't be located so precisely in a specific time; however, we are given clues about the span of time. Each story represents a brief flash in the protagonist's life, e.g. *What We Know Now* takes place over the course of the afternoon and evening of 31 December 1999. This compressed timeframe creates a sense of urgency and intensity while the narrator's frequent flashbacks extend the scope of each story, providing us with vital new information about his past.

### Present-tense first-person narration

The narrative is told in the first person, from the point of view of the nameless narrator. The use of the present tense lends immediacy to the action (e.g. 'Dad dodges cars quicker than usual' (p.9), not 'Dad *dodged* cars quicker than usual').

Although the narrator's personality is not particularly strong, the first-person perspective is vital. In an interview, Amsterdam explained why he used this technique:

> We would absolutely lose sympathy for [the narrator] if we didn't have the closest view into his conscience. Additionally, being trapped there is what keeps the book intimate and concerned with the conduct of people, rather than the apocalypse. (Meyer 2010)

The first-person perspective allows us to become emotionally engaged with the narrator and protagonist, even though he is deeply flawed. Because we are confined within his viewpoint, we receive exactly the same information that he does. We are, in other words, *trapped* within his vision of reality.

## Language

### Objective statement of events

The narrator's words are usually delivered in a flat, relatively expressionless tone that tends towards a basic statement of events. The voice shuns (avoids) drama, excessive description and flowery prose. A short example of the narrative style demonstrates this lack of drama:

> I'm looking at this root I've dug into and trying to figure out which plant it's from, if I've tasted it before, or if it's worth cutting off and giving it a try. I raise a shred of it to my nose to give it a sniff when my eye notices this guy stumbling towards me in the distance. (p.67)

This stripped-back, one-thing-after-another style works to eliminate all the potential drama in the passage in favour of straight realism. Instead of emphasising the heightened emotions of the situation, Amsterdam nearly always chooses to avoid directly expressing the narrator's feelings. We are therefore forced to think for ourselves about what other characters might be feeling, rather than being told what to think by the author.

### Humour as a coping mechanism

If there is one word that defines the tone of the narration, it would be 'deadpan'. Although the narrative is structured around traumatic events, the central character perhaps shows less emotion than would usually be expected of someone in his situation. While an apocalyptic novel might not seem like the most fertile ground for humour, *Things We Didn't See Coming* contains many funny elements.

The book's dark humour is often based around common anxieties about the future. The irreverent behaviour of children in contrast to the ultra-seriousness of the adults around them can also be amusing. For example, in *The Theft That Got Me Here*, the narrator refers to his grandmother, who has just emerged from a years-long coma, as 'Rip Van Winkle', a fairytale character who slept for 20 years (p.28). He retains this cheeky, laid-back attitude, even as the situation gets progressively grimmer.

The characters' frequently irrational attachment to the past provides amusement too. For example, when the grandfather's stolen car is in danger of being stolen *again* in *The Theft That Got Me Here*, he suddenly becomes possessive: 'Some man-and-his-car thing clicks and suddenly he's calling them every name he knows' (p.39). In *Predisposed*, the narrator humorously mocks Jeph for 'making a tough face that he probably stole from an old Western' (p.134). Throughout the book, people cling to useless items, attitudes and customs from a long-vanished world. Again, in *Dry Land*, the fussy, obsolete customs of the old world are played for laughs:

> Liz uncorks a half-empty bottle of white, hands it to me, and says a little too loud, 'Sorry, it's not chilled,' like it's hilarious. (p.52)

All of these examples refer to behaviour that is no longer appropriate, which is why they are funny.

There are also several examples of people acting inappropriately, given their situation. In *Dry Land*, when the narrator and the two women are stuck in a rainstorm, 'Liz starts belting out "Singin' in the Rain"' (p.53). In *Cakewalk*, although the protagonist's life has been placed in danger by a virus-ridden man, Margo's first instinct is to be funny. When she comes home to find her underwear tangled on the ground, she jokingly accuses the narrator of cross-dressing: 'I see her bra, twisted up in the dust. "Did you have a relaxing adventure with them in my absence?"' (p.77). Over and over, people deal with an almost unbearable reality in trivial or inappropriate ways.

Amsterdam represents black humour, or 'gallows humour', as a kind of coping mechanism. For example, in *Best Medicine*, the protagonist copes with his horrible job by inventing insulting nicknames for his terminally ill clients – 'The Octopus', 'The Pregnant Teen', 'The Shaky Widow', 'Machiavelli', 'The Miserable Couple', 'Magellan', 'The Young Man of Independent Means' – all of which help him deal with the morbid nature of his task.

This flippant tone has another purpose: it conceals the 'real' person. The narrator is quite sensitive, yet he doesn't want to reveal too much about himself to anyone else. By nastily labelling the people on the tour and ridiculing their need for spiritual guidance, the narrator is able to conceal his own need for love and healing. His detached, ironic tone is really a ruse (disguise); he is a far more sensitive person than he lets on.

# CHAPTER-BY-CHAPTER ANALYSIS

## What We Know Now

**Summary:** *The narrator's father attempts to prepare the family for a catastrophe.*

### Key points

This is the 'odd story out' in the collection, as it tells the story of a world that is much like our own.

The action begins frantically, on New Year's Eve 1999. At first, we don't know exactly what is happening. We're receiving events from a young child's limited perspective but he is unclear exactly what's going on.

The child's father, Otis, is packing the car ready to move away from the neighbourhood. An atmosphere of paranoia is rapidly created. The child vows to 'keep a lookout' (p.6), suggesting that the neighbours cannot be trusted. Cate, the child's mother, is unceremoniously introduced.

From the beginning the protagonist is confused and anxious; he admits that he is 'trying to figure out why Dad packed all the kitchen knives', and establishes an atmosphere of mistrust by concealing this from his mother (p.7). Hearing the adults talk around him, the boy doesn't seem to fully understand what is going on.

It gradually becomes clear that the father predicts that disaster is imminent, an assertion his wife doesn't believe. As the radio broadcasts New Year's Eve parties, Cate's mocking observation that 'London Bridge seems to be still standing. That's a good sign, isn't it?' (p.9) makes the father 'quiet and angry' (p.9). At this stage, the father seems to be dragging the family into disaster.

The father's collision with a woman's car on the freeway is pivotal. He drives on, obviously believing his own family's fate to be more important than that of the woman's. Shocked, Cate angrily accuses him of having 'done a hit and run' (p.12).

The grandparents' house is like another world. Compared to the father's apocalyptic visions of destruction, the grandmother signifies calm and rationality. 'Everything will be fine until it's not. Then we can worry', she tells the narrator (p.23). Meanwhile, the father continues to warn about society's imminent collapse, contemptuously describing humanity as 'A whole species that didn't think to set its clocks the right way' (p.22).

After the father leaves the party, the grandfather offers another 'voice of reason':

> It's always been the end of the world. What did we have this century? World War I, influenza, the Depression, World War II, concentration camps, the atomic bomb. Now he's scared about a computer glitch? A blackout? (p.16)

The boy goes outside to meet his father, as he 'has to get to Dad by midnight' (p.18). Their meeting has clearly been premeditated. The boy, believing in his father's predictions, knows that 'everyone will come out here looking for fresh water' after the crash. The father, preparing to desert his wife, reassures his son that 'we couldn't have taken her' (p.21) and finally shares the full extent of his vision with his son: 'the lights go out, the water shuts off, and you know in your heart that they're never coming back on. That's the future' (p.22). The chapter ends with father and son embracing.

When this chapter is read in isolation, Otis' insanity seems obvious. This chapter, then, seems like a psychological study of the effects of paranoia: the father, in the grip of a deranged fantasy, has destroyed his family, abandoned his wife, and perhaps permanently damaged his son.

***Q*** At what point does the father's insanity become obvious?

***Q*** Whose perspective is handled most sympathetically?

## The Theft That Got Me Here

***Summary:*** *The narrator and his grandparents attempt to escape the city.*

Tension and unease are created right from the opening of this story. The abrupt first sentence – 'The pills seem to be helping' (p.26) – raises several questions in the reader's mind. The following few sentences reveal a number of problems in the narrator's life: his grandmother is severely incapacitated; his grandfather has lost his driving licence; and the narrator now has a criminal record and 'delinquent friends' (p.26) of whom his mother strongly disapproves.

It is clear that all is not well in the wider society, too, because the family is using 'allotment coupons'. Gradually, the ever-present threat of scarcity and crime is revealed: 'Grandpa can get ripped off without leaving the house' (p.26) and the weather is 'so dusty' (p.27) that people don't go outside much anymore. Water scarcity has made it illegal to grow grass, but the narrator 'noticed a few law-breakers keeping tiny squares of lawn', and tells us that he has finished his water ration for the day (p.27). The only sign of 'nature' as we know it is in the grandfather's nature magazines featuring 'jungles and glaciers' (p.29), both of which presumably no longer exist. The world's natural resources are severely crippled.

Everything changes when the boy's grandmother, who has been 'off the map for six years', suddenly emerges from her coma. She makes breakfast, after asking the narrator to find food. He scrounges some milk and an egg 'after just half an hour of wandering around' (p.28).

## Key point

The unrealistic premise of the grandmother's recovery makes this story seem surreal, adding to its 'nightmare' quality.

Together, the grandparents decide to make the journey back to their 'old property' in the country (p.31). However, this will not be easy, as the environment has recently been segregated into 'city' and 'country'. People with 'urban' identity cards aren't allowed out.

Nevertheless, they resolve to escape. The grandmother, representing the voice of nostalgia, reminisces about a time when the 'entire nation' was doing well (p.31). Yet her idealised vision of the past exists only in her mind. At the country-city checkpoint, the grandmother cleverly tricks the inexperienced border guard into letting them through.

Suburbia has become a deserted wasteland. Everyone 'had to choose' between urban and rural during the mass evacuation (p.32). We learn that Grandma and Grandpa honeymooned in the 1960s, so we can deduce that the story must be set shortly before 2010. In other words, the author has created an alternative reality.

When the trio of city-dwellers are discovered by a gang of country-dwelling teenage girls, they are called 'godless freaks' and pelted with food (p.34). The country is clearly the food-producing centre of this society, as 'all the orchards and the factories' are there (p.34). The narrator's comment that many places are 'on barter' suggests the currency system has collapsed.

They find a stock of goods in a house. Forced to eat stolen goods due to hunger, the grandparents are quickly morally corrupted by scarcity, yet they still cling to their morality by pretending otherwise: 'even though they're eating [the food], they know it's stolen' (p.36). Soon, however, they collude with their grandson in stealing a car, quickly getting hooked on 'the thrill of larceny' (p.38). When their stolen car is ransacked, the grandfather is hypocritically disgusted (p.39).

The car they have stolen is an 'enormous mansion', a symbol of human wastefulness. Here, we learn of the grandparents' plan to get 'reclassified' as country-dwellers and live on their old country property (p.41). The whole story, then, can be seen as their attempt to reclaim their lost past.

After some time on the road, they check into a seedy hotel resembling a brothel. The protagonist, displaying his libido, casually notes that 'I'm going to hit on the blonde, and see if all the girls here are virgins as advertised or what', and drools over her 'come-fuck-me looks' (p.42). His casual objectification of women suggests that his moral degradation extends beyond mere theft.

The story's devastating ending highlights the impossibility of reclaiming the past in this inhospitable world. The grandmother soon falls back into her coma; as the protagonist drives back to the city, he feels as if he is taking them back 'to prison' (p.43). The story comes to a fitting close when he finds out that the grandfather has killed himself and his wife in the back seat.

Although the couple's escape attempt is temporarily uplifting, the tragic ending underscores the situation's hopelessness. In this world, it is no longer possible to leave your troubles behind – everything leads back to the 'prison' of poverty and destitution. The story ends with the protagonist planning to bury his grandparents and escape from the city on his own – perhaps indicating that there is still some hope left in his own actions.

***Q*** Is the grandfather's act defensible? Why or why not?

***Q*** What is the significance of the protagonist's pocketing of his dead grandparents' money at the end of the story?

## Dry Land

***Summary:*** *The narrator tries to evacuate a flooded house, encountering a mother and daughter who eventually try to kill him.*

### Key point

The story's central situation of the failed connection between human beings is repeated over and over in the novel.

The story starts off on an unexpected note: 'A rain horse is a horse that's been sensitised to travel in downpours without complaint' (p.46). The bone-dry world of the previous story seems to have vanished. This is a land of frequent and catastrophic flooding, with only a 'few dry months' per year (p.52).

The protagonist has been hired by Land Management people to protect the public from 'starvation and flooding' (p.46); however, children see him as a 'bogeyman' (p.47). His job – to evacuate people from their houses – makes him a figure of public fear and hatred. As in the previous story, he is not above looting repossessed houses.

The industrial collapse has advanced from the previous story. The narrator is pleased that he hasn't 'had to take [his] pistol out once' (p.48), and notes that 'the [electricity] grid went down' some time ago (p.49). There is a note of satisfaction in his voice as he mocks people's now-useless 'thousand dollar appliances' (p.49).

Although a government employee, the narrator is so hungry that he resorts to eating cushion foam (p.49). He wakes up to a woman, also starving, looming over him with a knife. She and her daughter have 'both got that pulled look in their cheeks, like food is a memory' (p.50).

He soon succeeds in calming the pair down. The mother is a drunk, surviving on the bottles left in the house, as 'there hasn't been a proper season for grapes in years' (p.52). Although the pair seems desperate, the narrator deduces that they once 'led a comfortable life' (p.52). As the protagonist and the daughter go foraging for food, he tries to convince the girl to leave her ailing mother and make a new life for herself. She refuses.

Back in the house, they contemplate burning photographs and even hair for warmth, signifying a distinct lack of sentimentality. The mother tries to seduce the protagonist, who is totally aware of her motivations for this, as 'she'll think that sleeping with me could save her house' (p.59). Although sex has become a kind of bargaining chip, sleeping with the mother still makes him momentarily happy: 'I'm not cold anymore because I've got a naked someone in my arms' (p.61).

The narrator's attempt to guide the women to safety fails when the mother shoots him with his own gun (p.63). Lying on the ground in what he presumes are his last moments, he has a vivid, poetic fantasy about a beautiful woman:

> I'm imagining the person who finds me. A real country woman, about my age, who can forgive this mutt. Let's give her crimson hair to her shoulders with freckled cheeks and sleeves rolled up above her hard-worked forearms. (pp.63–4)

The story ends with the protagonist lying wounded and abandoned on the ground.

***Q*** What do the mother's actions suggest about this new world's moral framework?

***Q*** Why do children see the narrator as a 'bogeyman' (p.47)?

## Cakewalk

**Summary:** *The narrator's life is endangered as he is approached by a plague-infected stranger.*

### Key point

There has been a long gap between this story and the last – we are not told how Margo and the narrator met, and we only learn about their time together in the city indirectly.

Like the previous story, this one takes place in a time of extreme environmental stress. Now, however, drought has returned. The narrator talks about 'digging up something to eat', as well as the need to 'dig for water' (p.66). Everything is parched. Just as the narrator tries to eat cushion filling in the previous story, here he tries to eat a tree root (p.67).

Disease has accompanied drought: the protagonist encounters a man coughing up blood under a tree and, quickly deciding that he is 'too close for safety' (p.68), waits for the man to die instead of helping him.

The protagonist is now reliant on Margo, who does the stealing for both of them. His admission that she 'always makes me feel safe' (p.69) suggests that traditional gender roles are reversed in this relationship. As in the last story, the narrator has the hated task of evacuating people from their homes.

This story is really about the rare event of two people coming into contact with one another. Even though all human contact is apparently extremely dangerous, the sick stranger urges him to 'let me finish talking to you', and tauntingly accuses him of being 'desperate to talk' (p.73).

When the man invades his tent, the protagonist has a moment of empathy for all the people from whom he has stolen in the past. 'I am done with stealing ... history has given us another road today' (p.75). The sight of his home being invaded forces him to empathise with others in a similar position, making this home invasion the turning point of his life.

When Margo returns, she finds him on the floor, helpless with sickness. Fearing the stranger's disease, the two flee 'before either of us gets any symptoms' (p.78). The narrator feels morally compromised by the incident, stating that 'I feel *fallen*' (p.78).

His decision to stop stealing is highly significant. The couple met while they were robbing a store, and their bond is based on theft. They are travelling towards a camp, where they plan to 'be the ghosts that feed off the edges' (p.80). He is relieved, however, when the supposedly 'empty' camp is in fact filled with people.

Due to the narrator's moral transformation, his act of desperation at the beginning of the story – eating wood – is transformed into a strange kind of redemption: 'The fibres separate like white meat from a chicken breast' (p.81), he says. It tastes sweet to him, precisely because *he didn't steal it.*

Just as he imagines being rescued by an almost angelic female figure in the previous story, here he imagines a marriage with a similarly idealised version of Margo:

> Silently, I ask her to marry me. I want it the way people used to do it – in the middle of a garden, in front of the family and friends with everyone still alive. A long wooden table filled with roasts and vegetables and cakes. Three nights of dancing and drinking on a hillside. (p.81)

His vision of marriage, like his hallucination of rescue in *Dry Land*, is intensely nostalgic. He is at least partly redeemed in this story, becoming 'strangely calm' because 'it's going to be different now' (p.82). His decision to move into the future as an honest man is vitally important.

***Q*** What does the story reveal about Margo's character?

## Uses for Vinegar

**Summary:** *While living inside a camp, Margo and the narrator decide to escape together.*

### Key point

Margo and the narrator's relationship has now broken down. However, she clearly still wields significant power over him, via her sexuality.

The environmental situation has obviously worsened further. People have 'run out of their houses' after the 'windstorms' and 'fires' (p.84). The constant rain in *Dry Land* has vanished.

The city centre visited by the protagonist has just been gutted by fire. Its fate is only mentioned briefly ('deep-ground oil drilling at the centre of town, compromised fault line, no rain in fourteen months, ignition' (p.85)), but this information is enough. The clearest example of environmental collapse is the plague of bugs 'with a one-inch stinger' (p.85). This introduced pest species has an excruciatingly painful bite, attacking people without warning.

The narrator's rival, Shane (also Margo's ex-boyfriend), works in rescue operations – a considerably more prestigious job than that of the narrator, who is still in charge of evictions (p.87). Even though he, Shane and Margo spend a lot of time together, he is 'the nervous guy in the triangle' (p.86), and fears losing her to Shane. Unfavourably comparing himself to Shane, the narrator worries that he is not a 'gallant knight' (p.88). The story therefore introduces an element of sexual rivalry absent in previous stories, making it close to a conventional romance.

The population of the village has been through severe trauma, and 'everyone is on some pill for coping' (p.90). In perhaps the most explicit mention of religion, the protagonist admits that 'I'm just not that enticed by the Kingdom of Heaven'; everyone else, though, is waiting for the 'second coming' (p.91).

The protagonist offers to escape from the camp with Margo after duping Shane, telling her that 'we'll be invisible' (p.93). Yet he is cynical about their chances. Beneath the hard-bitten facade, he has been 'longing for Margo', and proposes that the two of them escape from the camp in order to 'see what shape the coast is in' (p.97). The protagonist's story can be seen as a meditation on the power of hope: despite being a virtually broken man, he is sustained by the thought of Margo's presence.

When Margo fails to arrive at their meeting point, the narrator realises that he is 'a sucker' (p.96). The hope that has sustained him has evaporated. When she arrives at the last minute, 'She pulls me away from the crowd, locks her arms around me and we finally finally kiss' (p.98). This image would be more in place in a Hollywood film, and Margo knows it: 'Enough sentimental, let's get out of here', she says (p.98). The two of them, having ditched Shane, are successfully reunited.

***Q*** Why is so much attention paid to the bugs in the story?

## The Forest for the Trees

***Summary:*** *Margo and the narrator are befriended by a rich and exploitative political leader.*

### Key point

This is the first time we see how 'the other half lives': the lives of the ultra-rich are shockingly privileged. These stark social divisions make the conflict running through the novel unsurprising.

The narrator and Margo have become involved in a bizarre 'love triangle' with Juliet, a charismatic female political figure posing as a revolutionary leader.

Although all relationships must now be approved by the State, the protagonist claims that entering such a contract is 'almost like marriage' (p.100). He is still capable of romance, even in these unpromising circumstances. The protagonist has become Juliet's speechwriter. The couple, who have become part of her entourage, even visit 'her island' for a holiday (p.103).

Juliet markets herself as the leader of the disadvantaged: 'early on, during the urban/rural battles, she got famous by showing up at the front of all the protests' (p.104). The protagonist admits that 'I thought she was God' (p.105), suggesting that celebrity has replaced politics. In this future, just as in our own, celebrity has been elevated to a position that is virtually equivalent to godliness.

After Juliet meets the couple at a dance club, she takes them back to her unimaginably luxurious truck and hires them as sexual companions (p.106), wiping their criminal records as a courtesy (p.107). The protagonist tells us that Juliet 'dressed me up in rubber and had me fuck her on the main stage of just about every flesh club' (p.107–8). The couple live out a depraved fantasy existence with the amoral Juliet.

As the narrative progresses, we learn about the protagonist's increasing sense of disillusionment amidst great wealth. They now have *everything* – including access to Juliet's wine, 'Viognier from her vineyards' (p.112), and exquisite greenhouse-bred food. Yet he is aware that moral boundaries have been sheared away: 'Name an act, a theft, a drug, a social rung, a job, a dream: we have tried it or abstained only for reasons of health or sanity or law' (p.112). Morality is no longer a part of their world.

The narrative ends with the deliberate burning of the countryside by the two women. Deeply disillusioned, the narrator observes:

> I look at the women, their excited faces shining from all our layers of fireproof glass, and realise I no longer want anything at all. (p.120)

The Senator's lust for power finds an outlet in pure destruction, an impulse that Margo gladly shares. Only the protagonist's repulsed reaction offers some faint hope.

***Q*** What motivates the women's joint act of arson?

## Predisposed

***Summary:*** *Now separated from Margo, the protagonist is made guardian of a teenage boy.*

### Key point

This is perhaps the most 'traditional' of the stories, and the most positive treatment of human relationships. Only necessity severs the connection between the narrator and Jeph.

The protagonist, now aged 36, is living in a small rural community that resembles an Amish village. Margo has disappeared. He has been made guardian of a teenager, Jeph, who is (grudgingly) helping him with the chores. Jeph is doted on, as, due to the fertility crisis, children are rare. He displays a disrespectful attitude, boasting about being able to 'jerk off' (p.124), walking with an 'exaggerated swagger' (p.124), and jokingly calling his guardian 'Faggot' (p.124) (also the term for a bundle of sticks, which explains the joke). All in all, Jeph and the protagonist have a fairly typical father/son relationship. This is the endpoint of the social breakdown warned about by the father in the first story: as a response to environmental pressures, the world has broken down into small communities.

We find out more and more about the people's dire state as we progress. Half of the tribe are in the cemetery (p.126). Jeph longs to escape from the village, but the narrator in turn longs to escape from Jeph: 'in two years he'll be sixteen and I'll be free from him' (p.127).

Searching Jeph's room, the protagonist finds a sheet containing his entire medical history. Realising he 'could lose guardianship' if the search is discovered, he covers his tracks – but not before finding out that he is sterile, probably from the virus contracted in *Cakewalk* (p.129).

Everything else about the village suggests that the world's industrial base has been destroyed, and technology has regressed. The tasks that the villagers engage in are more akin to a society of peasants than of an advanced civilisation: they 'strain the yoghurt' (p.126), and later they are 'weaving sticks and grass together and sealing it with clay' (p.131). Eventually, Jeph urges the protagonist to 'take action' by escaping from the village (p.133).

Outside the village, all that exists is a 'dusty strip of roadside farms, all growing the same spindly, shadowy crop' (p.134). Food shortages are ever-present. The two argue about driving, just like a father and son would; the brittle bond between them is quite touching.

When they visit the doctor's, it is revealed that the protagonist has cancer as a result of UV exposure. In a fatherly tone, the narrator reassures Jeph: 'In ten years' time you'll run the place – if everyone's not dead, of course. A pleasant way to end up, a farmer, a collectivist. Isolationist, I think that's called' (p.138). His father's advice in the first chapter, i.e. that humanity will 'fall apart from interdependence' (p.13), has become reality.

The arrival at the doctor's surgery is a revelation for Jeph; starved of sexually available women, he stares at the nurse 'in horny wonder' (p.136). As the protagonist finds out that he has cancer, Jeph is given 'a little fix-it for his puberty' (p.137). Clearly, the sight of a teenager entering puberty is a rare sight in this world, where the population is rapidly ageing and fertility has catastrophically declined.

The pair enters the city, which resembles a vision of Hell: 'a brown haze is already visible, the nondescript skyline growing there like skin cancer' (p.139) – the metaphorical cancer of the city mirrors the literal cancer with which the protagonist has just been diagnosed.

The protagonist, realising that he must leave Jeph to fend for himself, opens the car door and escapes. Suddenly alone, Jeph waits for him to return before finally driving off alone (p.140).

***Q*** Are the narrator's reasons for leaving Jeph convincing?

## The Profit Motive

***Summary:*** *The protagonist is auditioned for the provisional government.*

### Key point

This story shows the greatly compromised way in which societies choose to deal with their problems. The unelected provisional government is heavily undemocratic, although this might be necessary under the circumstances.

This story presents a uniquely apocalyptic vision of reality. Having escaped from the rural compound, the narrator becomes ensconced in a highly organised gated community.

The environment has deteriorated further. There is no more rain, a feature carried over from the earlier stories. However, there *is* some superficially positive news, that 'the country has stability again' (p.144). The uniforms of the people are reminiscent of those of Ancient Rome, perhaps giving the impression of a less democratic age.

Once inside the camp, the protagonist is given a series of tests to see if he is suitable leadership material. While being interviewed by a woman, he is tempted to betray others in order to get the leadership position, yet refuses. The woman, Karuna, pretends to be offended by his refusal to be bribed.

Having undergone the interview, the protagonist is put before a panel of judges. They approve of his past conduct, noting that he has 'consistently, where practicable, worked for [his] living, in both rural and urban communities' (p.156). He also refuses to tell the other members of the committee that Karuna has attempted to bribe him – which is lucky, because this turns out to be a test of his character. He is asked to defend the citizens 'with the goal of the social good' (p.157), a demand to which he agrees.

For the duration of the interview, the protagonist is monitored for his emotional response via a strangely beautiful technique: 'an abstract pink and blue image of my body ... the colours throb with reddish pulses radiating out from my centre' (p.158). He gets the job.

***Q*** Is Karuna's character sympathetic? Why or why not?

## Best Medicine

***Summary:*** *The narrator, now terminally ill, reunites with his father.*

### Key point

It is difficult to tell whether this represents a 'religious' ending signifying hope, or an example of the protagonist being conned by his father.

In the final story, the protagonist is 40 years old, now a tour guide for the terminally ill. Although he is surrounded by squalor, he still desires to 'heal each of my cells with love' (p.164).

We soon learn that he has resolved to see his father, whom he has not seen since he was 15 (p.166). Desperate now, he is tempted to try his father's unorthodox healing methods. The father's situation is enviable:

> Sometime before the Barricades started, Dad bought ten acres in the mountains and started building his outpost, with safe water, safe air and a monumentally secure garden. A kind of paradise really. (p.166)

His father, a modern version of a hippie who rejects the products of industrial civilisation, has succeeded in creating a new 'Garden of Eden'. In the process, he has also become a kind of religious figure.

When the narrator and his patients arrive at his father's property, he has become virtually indistinguishable from the diseased. It seems at first that he is taking the patients to be healed by his father, who is also his final hope. Soon it is the protagonist's turn to be 'saved' by his eccentric father. The book ends on a strange and unexpected note of peace:

> I suddenly realise that it's better here with him than anywhere I've been. I could live like this. I want to tell him what I know now, that I'm going to stay and take care of him. (p.174)

The novel's last words are 'he closes my eyes' (p.174). However, we don't know whether this represents the protagonist's death. No matter what the significance of the final paragraph, it is clear that the protagonist has made peace with his father in some fundamental way.

The note of acceptance at the end of the piece is difficult to interpret: is it ironic or genuine? Contacting his father appears to have fundamentally changed the protagonist. By surrendering, he has succeeded in making human contact under incredibly compromised circumstances.

# CHARACTERS & RELATIONSHIPS

## The Protagonist/Narrator

**Key quote**

'Now is as good a time as any to change.' (p.79)

The central character of the novel is unusual for a number of reasons. Most importantly, his lack of a name signifies his identity as an 'Everyman' figure, i.e. someone who symbolises the whole of humanity. His chief function is to bear witness to events, and relay them to us. By taking on a wide variety of jobs, he is able to provide us with information about many different aspects of his society.

One of the protagonist's main characteristics is his dual personality. We see him change from the vulnerable boy of *What We Know Now* into the tough, hard-bitten survivor of the later stories. The dishonesty and ruthlessness that is required to survive in this ravaged world gradually eats away at his peace of mind. After leaving his parent figures, he begins a long, lonely journey through the landscape that places huge physical and emotional demands on him.

Cracks soon appear in his tough-guy persona. Although the emotionally damaged protagonist often talks about sex, he is really looking for love. He never really seems to recover from the separation from his parents and grandparents, and is always acutely aware of his isolation.

The major struggle that goes on within the protagonist's soul is his resistance to theft as a way of life. This may strike us as a little odd: after all, isn't it understandable that someone would want to steal food so that they can survive? But the issue is a lot more important to the narrator, who experiences theft as a persistent and immoral temptation. By leaving Margo at the end of *The Forest for the Trees*, he takes a major step toward liberating himself from this compromised mode of existence.

## The Father (Otis)

**Key quote**

'What's the right amount of worry?' (p.22)

The narrator's enigmatic father is difficult to decipher. Featuring only in the novel's first and last chapters, the father is viewed by his son with a strong mixture of admiration and condemnation. It is unclear how we are to judge him – is he a fraud, or a prophet?

In *What We Know Now*, the father seems paranoid, dominating and controlling. He will go to any lengths to control his family's lives, and is utterly convinced that society is about to be destroyed. The father's extreme, doom-laden visions inevitably alienate other family members, apart from his trusting son. His wife, for example, has been ruthlessly pushed aside in the mad rush to prepare for the worst.

But the picture is more complex, as the father clearly cares deeply for his son. When they are reunited in the forest in *What We Know Now*, he says that 'it's good to see my boy' (p.20). The final words to his son are 'I'm sorry' (p.23); similarly, at the end of the story, he 'hugs [his son] as tight as he can' (p.23). However, the fact that he clearly has his child's best interests at heart is compromised by his apparent insanity.

Subsequent chapters force the reader to reassess the father's behaviour: if he was *right* about the Y2K Bug, he could be right about everything else. This revised perception makes the father a doomed and heroic figure, rather than a malicious and insane one.

So, how are we to judge him? One thing is clear: he is not a saint. He may have been right about the environmental problems facing the world, but he is not necessarily morally admirable. In the final story, the more negative aspects of the father's personality emerge: there is a whiff of the conman about him. His efforts to establish himself as a kind of 'guru' make the narrator extremely sceptical:

> The path is decorated with all sorts of tribal hoo-hahs. Sticks tied to rocks (with braids of silver hair from my father's ridiculous mane, no doubt) and stuck in the ground to ward off evil, welcome friends, whatever he's in the mood for. (pp.170–1)

This perspective is one of unmitigated cynicism, held by a man who once loved and respected his father.

Yet his desperate need to be loved eventually leads to his submission to his father's 'healing' ritual. It is difficult to tell whether the father's character is vindicated by this final scene. Although the son eventually undergoes the healing procedure at his father's hands, it is doubtful whether his father's extreme measures were legitimate or necessary. As a 'healer', he has clearly made a lot of money from other people's suffering.

## The Mother (Cate)

**Key quote**

'If you'd just get something like a plan back into your life you wouldn't be so paranoid and scattered, and things would work again.' (p.10)

Although we know little about the narrator's mother, she seems like a balanced, rational person who simply fails to understand the signs of future danger.

The first story describes a decent woman who has become increasingly frustrated by her husband's alarmism. The protagonist's habit of calling her by her first name signifies his disrespect for her, in comparison to his father. Yet although she is wrong about the future, she clearly does all she can to keep her family together under difficult circumstances. Her longest speech to her son is revealing:

> I don't want you to learn one thing from tonight. Not about how to conduct yourself during times of stress, not about how to respect other people, not about how to manage your own insane worries. I want you to look out the window and watch the trees go by, because that's what I intend to do. (p.12)

Here, Cate gives the admirable impression of a mother who is trying to ignore the worst excesses of her husband's behaviour while ensuring that her son receives a moral education. Yet, like the grandparents, Cate belongs to the 'old world' (which is also the *reader's* world). Her methods of coping are inadequate for life's harsh new realities, and her efforts to protect her son break down when city life becomes too difficult.

After the narrator's 'dad left' (p.70), he 'toughed it out in the city' with his mother during his 15th year (p.166). Cate leaves after the narrator's departure to live in a desert town, where she trains to learn 'bullshit manners' as a servant for the rich (p.113). In *The Forest for the Trees*, the narrator tells us that he and Margo saw his mother 'two years ago' for 'the last time' (p.113). He mentions a hiking trip that he, Cate and Margo went on, during which they ran out of water: it is unclear whether his mother died on this trip, or some time shortly afterwards. An optimist to the very end, Cate maintains her false belief that Margo will 'save' the narrator from a life of crime (p.113).

The protagonist shows few signs of missing her, suggesting that their relationship was never particularly close. However, it is unclear whether this is because he is repressing his longing for her: we simply don't know enough about his inner thoughts to know for sure. It is also possible that his visions of the 'perfect woman' are connected to his need for a mother figure, a role the criminally inclined Margo is incapable of fulfilling.

## The Grandparents

**Key quote**

'We'll be one hundred per cent fine.' (p.15)

Like Cate, the protagonist's grandparents are representatives of the 'old world'. They do not understand what is going on in their environment, and they deal with their problems in a heartbreakingly futile way. The couple seem alarmingly – even comically – ignorant of what's really going on. In *What We Know Now*, for example, the grandfather says: 'Let's go about our business. We'll enjoy our hot chocolate and Baileys. [Your father] knows what he's missing and he can come in here whenever he likes' (p.16). These quaint, comforting yet utterly obsolete words throw full light on the grandparents' ignorance of the world's horrible new reality.

When things start going wrong, the grandparents are thrown into a society for which they are utterly unsuited. After the grandmother awakes from her years-long coma, the pair embarks on a doomed, farcical *Bonnie and Clyde*–style stealing spree with the protagonist. As the grandmother slips back into her coma, the grandfather chooses to end both their lives rather than go on living without hope.

Despite their tragic end, and their unpreparedness for the new world, the grandparents are positive characters. The grandmother, in particular, uses her charm to get through in the harsh world in which she finds herself. Trying to charm the guard at the gates of the city, she calls him a 'sweet man' (p.31), displaying courtesy that is virtually absent from the rest of the novel. The grandfather, while gruffer than his wife, is clearly concerned about her welfare. Given his clear attachment to her, his final act – killing his wife and himself – becomes far more sympathetic. The couple are *anachronistic*, i.e. they seem to exist in the wrong era. Their gentle, formal and meticulous behaviour seems utterly foreign to the merciless new world in which they find themselves.

## Liz and Jenna

### Key quotes

Liz: 'Why're you helping us? Shouldn't you be busy pushing us out the door?' (p.57)

Jenna: 'I'll take whatever you find that's edible, but I've got to chew it or I'll go out of my mind.' (p.53)

The mother and daughter encountered by the protagonist in *Dry Land* are two more pathetic relics of the 'old world', clinging together to ward off death. The hardships faced by the mother have made her unable to support her daughter. Traumatised, she drinks incessantly to escape the present.

Both women, having come from a 'comfortable life', are unable to cope with poverty (p.52). Neither woman possesses the resilience to deal with changed circumstances; both escape into fantasy and delusion. The mother, knowing perfectly well that she is no longer capable of caring for her daughter, admits that 'it's only me doing the drinking' (p.52). The narrator, when deciding whether to rescue Jenna, acknowledges that the mother would only become a burden: 'Liz will wander outside and be dead of exposure within two days, guaranteed' (p.56).

The protagonist's relationship with the mother and daughter is ambivalent. Sometimes he clearly needs them as much as they need him. The narrator is obviously comforted by the mother's presence – 'I'm not cold anymore because I've got a naked someone in my arms' (p.61) – yet it is clear that his need for company could be satisfied by anyone. He has no specific attachment to either person: his willingness to separate them if necessary suggests that he sees them as part of his job, rather than as human beings with their own needs.

The narrator coldly plans to take the daughter with him and leave the mother behind to die; they have been plotting to kill him all along. The mother and daughter's defences are crude and brutal, but their core of mutual love helps them survive dire circumstances. In an odd sort of a way, then, the mother's willingness to kill the narrator suggests hope, as it shows the lengths that she is prepared to go to in order to protect her daughter.

## Margo

**Key quote**

'Imagine how cool that would look? The three of us. Imagine. Imagine.' (p.118)

Margo, a mercurial (difficult to pin down) and deeply flawed character, represents the main object of the narrator's love. At first, it is difficult to see why he is attracted to her; however, it may be because of the security she offers. He admits that 'she always makes me feel safe', while 'she feels plenty safe on her own' (p.69).

Margo's most striking characteristic is her willingness to steal and lie without feeling remorse. In this sense, she is unworthy of the narrator's love. The protagonist sticks with her because he needs someone – anyone – to love. He disapproves of Margo's stealing sprees, though, and tries valiantly to help her give up her life of crime. In this sense, Margo is the protagonist's chief source of temptation, dragging him back to the dishonest life he tries to leave behind.

It is unclear whether Margo is *immoral* (someone who knowingly violates moral codes) or simply *amoral* (a person with no morals whatsoever). The narrator is the moral guide of the two, while she is the pragmatist whose ruthlessness helps them survive. In *Cakewalk*, the protagonist's desire to become honest is short-lived; she soon drags him back to a 'fallen' life of theft.

Margo's willingness to betray others to get ahead is shown often. In *Uses for Vinegar*, Margo has left the protagonist for another man, Shane, yet she subsequently bribes the protagonist with the promise of sex, betraying Shane so that they can elope together. Margo's betrayal is itself ambiguous, as it's unclear whether she does it to simply get ahead, or because she genuinely loves the protagonist.

Another layer of Margo's character is unveiled in *The Forest for the Trees*, when she shows a clear enthusiasm for their mutually exploitative relationship with the wealthy, amoral Juliet. While the protagonist is anguished at this sordid arrangement, Margo does not share his scruples.

The protagonist's fantasies about his 'ideal woman' indirectly shed light on Margo's character. These are *not* sexual fantasies, but rather the expressions of a yearning for a more exalted type of love that she can't provide. Margo can perhaps be considered a symbol of the fallen, imperfect world in which the protagonist is forced to live against his wishes. The fact that we last see her performing an act of arson provides a clue to the destructive nature of her personality.

## Juliet

**Key quote**

'If you want the rainbow, you've got to have some rain.' (p.114)

Juliet illustrates perfectly the future world's endemic (widespread) corruption. She is a politician with absolutely no empathy for her supporters: although she speaks the language of the 'people's struggle', she cares only about her own pleasure. Juliet can perhaps be interpreted as an allegory of our current political disengagement, or as Amsterdam's comment on the level of political corruption in our society. Having been converted into a cult figure by her admirers, the pure figurehead Juliet is obviously only in politics for the money and fame.

Her character also reveals the intimate connection between hedonism (love of pleasure) and destruction. As an extremely wealthy individual, she is able to wreak destruction on a vast scale. Despite having unheard-of wealth, Juliet tries to get her 'kicks' by indulging in more and more dangerous or deviant fantasy behaviour. Emotions such as kindness or compassion seem utterly foreign to her, while people are simply possessions to be toyed with before being discarded.

Juliet also represents the forces of privatisation, and the dissolving of the 'social contract', a term which refers to citizens' willingness to give up some of their personal rights in exchange for receiving protection by the law (see *Themes, Ideas and Values*). Everything about her depends on private wealth – her private vineyards, cars, gadgets and servants provide her with a level of luxury that would shock her impoverished supporters.

There is therefore not much to Juliet beyond her basic appetites. We never find out anything about her inner thoughts at all; we only know that she loves pleasure for its own sake. She has everything, yet she is scarcely a full human being, suggesting that obscene wealth can damage one's capacity for human feeling.

## Jeph

### Key quotes

'I'm in fine shape.' (p.125)

'What I don't get is why does everyone here lie to each other all the time.' (p.132)

In many ways, Jeph is a typical teenager. Smart-mouthed, hyperactive and insolent, he treats his foster father – the narrator – with an even mixture of contempt and affection.

Obviously, Jeph benefits greatly from the fact that he is one of the last children left. The fertility crisis has peaked by the time of his appearance; children have become objects of veneration, enjoying almost total freedom. As all the adults around Jeph suffer from declining fertility, Jeph sees his ensuing puberty as proof of his superiority.

None of Jeph's faults are very bad ones, making him one of the most positive characters in the book. We expect such behaviour from teenagers, and although Jeph is quite rude, he is never malicious. Clearly too 'cool' to directly express his love for his guardian, he risks severe punishment by stealing the narrator's medical records in order to prolong his life.

As Jeph's cocky, sure-footed attitude is balanced by his far more positive characteristics, much of the book's hope resides with him. His seemingly negative acts – such as his theft of the protagonist's medical records – are done to ensure that the protagonist remains healthy. Jeph is almost a younger version of the protagonist, as his relationship with the narrator mirrors the father-son bond described in the first story.

The blissful interlude in which the narrator teaches Jeph how to drive harks back to the 'old world', and clarifies the narrator's fatherly feelings for Jeph. Later, the narrator affectionately comments on Jeph's attitude of 'horny wonder' (p.136), perhaps remembering his own teenage years. Although the narrator eventually escapes from Jeph's commune, the bond between the two is extremely touching while it lasts.

## Karuna

**Key quote**

'Understand this: you are completely, and I mean *completely*, among friends here.' (p.152)

Karuna dominates *The Profit Motive*, yet we know very little about her. She has significant power over the narrator, as he must submit to an interview with her in order to gain a government position.

Her story about the death of her family is taken by the narrator as a sign of her vulnerability. This positive, bright, and even at times flirtatious character tests the narrator's honesty by offering him a bribe, which he (luckily) refuses.

Karuna's deceptive 'testing' of the narrator's moral fibre is a major breach of trust. People rarely succeed in breaking through the narrator's defences as she is able to, and he is not duped again. His refusal to trust others is rewarded, however, when he finds out their interview is being observed. He is 'proud now that [he] refrained from a second dip into the goody box' (p.157), and passes the final test by refusing to 'dob in' Karuna for her attempted bribe. The final line of the story, where Karuna lets out a 'nasty little snort' (p.159), suggests that she is more ruthless than she seems.

# THEMES, IDEAS & VALUES

## Climate change and environmental catastrophe

**Key quote**

> 'Through the tinted glass is a field of tall, thin trees – just the trunks with their few spindly branches, all the colour of coal, and dead from thirst.' (p.110)

The changed climate is the defining aspect of Amsterdam's alternative world. The novel's physical environment is far less suitable for human habitation than the present one. Amsterdam attacks the myth that climate change is simply another example of apocalyptic paranoia.

The book is structured around the rapidly changing climate, which deteriorates substantially in each chapter. A brief summary of the different climates featured in the novel follows.

- *What We Know Now* takes place in 1999: climate has not yet become an issue.
- In *The Theft That Got Me Here,* things have changed: drought has begun to undermine food security, forcing people to use 'allotment coupons' (p.26). Everything is 'dusty', and people aren't allowed to keep 'tiny squares of lawn' (p.27).
- In *Dry Land,* the climate has mutated into a pattern of endemic flooding. The protagonist and his 'rain horse' travel through 'miles of flooded farmland', and he notes that each year only has a 'few dry months' (p.52). This flooding has had an equally devastating effect on the region's agriculture: the characters are reduced to eating rats, and the girl laments that they eat 'whatever we could find growing in the wild' (p.55).
- In *Cakewalk,* the rain is gone, setting the pattern of permanent drought that remains for the rest of the novel. The story takes place in a scrubby, arid space, where the protagonist is forced to collect water from a 'water pit' (p.67).
- In *Uses for Vinegar,* incessant heat has further degraded the climate. The protagonist speaks of 'windstorms' and 'fires' (p.84), and it is

clear that substantial environmental decline has taken place since the previous story.

- In *The Forest for the Trees,* these unforgivingly dry conditions continue. The protagonist has to 'take something for the UV', and complains of the 'unforgiving sun' (p.108). They long for the 'return of seasons' in this 'parched land' (pp.115–16).
- In *Predisposed,* continued drought-related agricultural failures have forced survivors to band together in small, self-sufficient communities. The protagonist describes passing a 'dusty strip of roadside farms, all growing the same spindly, shadowy crop' (p.134); all plants that are cultivated have to be 'environment-resistant' to cope with the heat and drought (p.139).
- In *The Profit Motive,* these environmental conditions have caused widespread destruction. He speaks of 'border clashes, the flu, the weather, and all the migrations they caused' (p.142). The result of this sustained climate catastrophe is mass social upheaval and human misery.
- In *Best Medicine,* the heat and UV – aided by a chain of erupting volcanoes – have become so uncontrollable that the protagonist has to wear 'coverup cream to smooth down the dark orange patches' of his skin cancers (p.170). When he meets his father again, he is amazed that 'Dad's not wearing anything protective' (p.171). Even brief exposure to the raging sun can be hazardous.

The damage is never explicitly linked to climate change, but the conditions of Amsterdam's Earth closely track those expected by climate change experts. For example, in *Requiem for a Species,* Clive Hamilton warns:

> Within the next several years enough warming will be locked into the system to set in train feedback processes that will overwhelm any attempts we make to cut back on our carbon emissions. We will be powerless to stop the jump to a new climate on Earth, one much less sympathetic to life. The kind of climate that has allowed civilisation to flourish will be gone and humans will enter a long struggle just to survive. (Hamilton 2010, p.2)

The situation Hamilton envisages is vividly dramatised in *Things We Didn't See Coming*.

Amsterdam's book also covers the connection between climate change and conflict. With the environmental base degraded to such a massive extent, nothing can stop rival powers becoming hostile towards each other and engaging in 'might makes right' behaviour. The book clearly suggests that our current way of life is unsustainable.

## Political systems

**Key quote**

'All of our nation-partners and an eager explosion of committees are working hard to make the new government viable.' (p.142)

Amsterdam implies that democracy is threatened when everyday life becomes exceedingly difficult. In *The Forest for the Trees*, for example, a popular city uprising is co-opted by Juliet, a charming, photogenic, yet emotionally exploitative figure who is utterly indifferent to the disadvantaged people she is supposed to be representing.

Amsterdam thus implies that the democratic institutions on which we rely are extremely fragile. In the hands of a pleasure-seeking celebrity, 'the government [in the novel] becomes more and more autocratic' (Antrim 2010). While the government seems to be fairly democratic in the novel's early stages, this soon decays into an oppressive oligarchy ('rule of the few') run by a small number of chosen people.

One of the book's major concerns, especially in *The Forest for the Trees*, is how politicians exploit the public. Juliet takes advantage of the downtrodden, enjoying immense personal wealth (including 'her island' and 'her vineyards') while posing as a saviour of the people. Although she 'got famous by showing up at the front of all the protests' (p.104), her concern is manufactured.

Part of the problem, Amsterdam suggests, is the extent to which the elite has sheltered itself from the environmental effects of its restrictive actions. Society becomes fragmented into a tiny elite able to retreat to its own gated communities and live off its privately-owned resources, and a massive, impoverished underclass.

## Retaining morality under extreme pressure

**Key quote**

'We didn't steal within the building – karma, etc.' (p.68)

The book clearly illustrates the difficulty of being generous towards others during times of extreme hardship.

'Old-fashioned morality' is represented by the protagonist's grandparents, especially in the second chapter. Although they are running low on food, the grandparents eat stolen food only reluctantly: 'Even though they're eating it, they know it's stolen. I'm the disappointment they're stuck with' (p.37). Yet by the end of the story, they too have become part of the system they previously despised. They steal a car soon after, despite having 'never felt the thrill of larceny before' (p.38). The fact that the grandparents – the last representatives of official morality – feel obliged to steal suggests that the 'old order' has collapsed.

Characters often sink to remarkable depths in the novel. For example, in *Dry Land*, the mother warns the protagonist, 'Don't screw her unless she wants!' (p.53). The fact that she is willing to entrust her daughter to a potential rapist is a chilling testament to her desperation.

## Declining fertility

**Key quote**

'Sexually mature now, if you can call it that, he's stuck out here with no outlet at all and younger than everyone by at least fifteen years.' (p.123)

The special treatment Jeph receives points to his privileged status as a child at a time of plummeting fertility. Amsterdam himself has commented that 'sperm counts are already about 50 per cent of what they were in the 1930s' (Cunningham 2010). It is interesting to note that declining fertility is a common theme in science fiction films. In the recent film *Children of Men* (2006), for example, the collapse of society is explicitly linked to the collapse of fertility and, for the film's narrator, the end of all hope:

> I can't really remember when I last had any hope, and I certainly can't remember when anyone else did either. Because really, since women stopped being able to have babies, what's left to hope for? (Cuarón 2006)

Themes of infertility and hopelessness are similarly interconnected in *Things We Didn't See Coming*:

> [Jeph] thinks his presence is a gift. The elders encouraged free participation by the children and now that he's the last survivor of the kids, he hasn't heard the word 'no' in a while. (p.122)

Both works use infertility as a symbol of human decline, suggesting that without fertility, there is no hope for the future.

## Religion – the death of God and exile from Eden

**Key quote**

'This is not about God, it's about me and the way I want to live and die.' (p.79)

Religion is an unspoken presence in *Things We Didn't See Coming*. It often seems as if God has abandoned this world, or is looking down on it mockingly. In *Cakewalk*, when the protagonist is confronted by a man infected with a virus, he hears 'some long tirade against people, including God' (p.68). There is a genuine sense in the novel that God has deserted this world.

Subtle religious references permeate the book. In *Cakewalk*, the protagonist notes:

> I have not, repeat, have not, found religion, but life has presented itself in these stark terms I feel *fallen*. And what else am I left to think? – with the two of us as we are now, lugging our water; fleeing, permanently banished from everywhere. (p.78)

Even though the narrator denies that this inner struggle has anything to do with God, it is framed in terms that could be interpreted as religious.

Further on, his use of the word 'fallen' contains clear biblical resonances. In the Bible, 'fallen' (i.e. 'having sinned') is specifically used to refer to the fate of Adam and Eve after they were exiled from Eden:

> And the LORD God said, Behold, the man is become as one of us, to know good and evil; and now, lest he put forth his hand, and take also of the tree of life, and eat, and live for ever: Therefore the LORD God sent him forth from the garden of Eden, to till the ground from whence he was taken. (Genesis 3:22–4)

Here, as in Genesis, humanity seems to have been exiled from its 'natural', or ideal, environment, creating a clear parallel between biblical exile and current reality. (The grandparents' unsuccessful journey to Bell's Brook, the place where they were married, in *The Theft That Got Me Here*, is another reference to the human desire to retreat to a perfect 'golden age', removed from strife and suffering.)

There is also reference to Noah's flood, a catastrophe that was intended to cleanse the Earth of its corrupt inhabitants in the Bible. In *Dry Land*, the narrator surveys a flooded and devastated landscape, as he and his horse go 'through miles of flooded farmland' to 'evacuate whoever's still thinking the sky's about to clear' (p.46). The biblical overtones of his description are apparent if we compare the similarly dramatic language found in Genesis:

> And the flood was forty days upon the earth; and the waters increased, and bare up the ark, and it was lift up above the earth. And the waters prevailed, and were increased greatly upon the earth; and the ark went upon the face of the waters. (Genesis 7:17–18)

This resemblance is intentional, as Amsterdam himself refers to the flood as 'Biblical' (Meyer 2009). The flood described in the Bible was induced by God to remove the sinners from the face of the Earth; in a sense, the flood in *Dry Land* seems to sweep away the corrupt world that we have seen in *The Theft That Got Me Here*. After the flood has taken place, the sophisticated institutions that have been built up in Chapter 2 gradually disintegrate. By the end of the book, society has reached a 'purer' state of self-contained outposts.

There are other biblical references. The many environmental hardships visited on the inhabitants – for example, the vile stinging insects in *Uses for Vinegar* – resemble the plagues unleashed by God on the Egyptians as punishment for their treatment of the Israelites:

> There came a grievous swarm of flies into the house of Pharaoh, and into his servants' houses, and into all the land in Egypt: the land was corrupted by reason of the swarm of flies. (Exodus 8:24)

The presence of God is a vexed issue. By the end of the book, it seems as if the supernatural God has given way to the figure of the guru, the narrator's father, who has established himself as a secular (non-religious) divinity. The protagonist's final trial can be seen as a kind of religious ceremony, in which he is 'blessed' by his father's healing ritual. Yet the book is ambiguous, as we don't know whether he genuinely believes in his father's healing ability.

## Epiphanies

**Key quote**

'For a moment, I feel that space she's always talking about, like I'm holding onto this world by a string.' (p.173)

The relentlessly depressing action of the novel is broken up by several *epiphanies* (spiritual revelations). The most striking occurs at the end of the second chapter, when the narrator imagines being discovered by a beautiful woman:

> I'm imagining the person who finds me. A real country woman, about my age, who can forgive this mutt. What else? Let's give her crimson hair to her shoulders with freckled skin and sleeves rolled up above her hard-worked forearms. She does what needs to be done and keeps a smile through it all, a sincere one. (p.64)

Ironically, the woman he *does* fall in love with is an unreformed thief who certainly does not live up to this beautiful vision. Yet the narrator consoles himself with these unsullied fantasy visions of pure happiness.

The device of epiphany is often used in literature to suggest a character's liberation from his or her circumstances. The epiphanies in *Things We Didn't See Coming* allow the protagonist to see the error of his own ways.

Much of the book concerns the protagonist's efforts to become an honest man, although he gets off to a fairly bad start. In *The Theft That Got Me Here*, his theft of a laptop computer initially earns him the contempt of his grandparents; however, as he matures, the protagonist continually seeks to atone for his past. At one point, he explicitly claims that he will give up stealing: 'History is giving us another road today ... we're going to be honest people' (p.75). The protagonist's unending, against-the-odds struggle to remain honest makes him almost heroic.

## Pessimism versus optimism about human nature

**Key quote**

> 'Look at us, surviving out here, two city kids. We can build things, we're resourceful, we can work with people.' (p.75)

There is a constant struggle in the book between the forces of cynicism and optimism. At first glance, the narrative seems unfailingly pessimistic, as it depicts the Earth's environment undergoing catastrophic meltdown.

However, the pessimistic interpretation is tempered by a clear strand of optimism about humanity's ability to cope. A key comparison is with Cormac McCarthy's novel *The Road*, which is also bleak, yet contains a similar faith in human resilience. Like *Things We Didn't See Coming, The Road* features a man on a journey through a blighted landscape. Despite enduring violence and starvation, the father in *The Road* fully recognises the importance of survival. He urges his son to 'carry the fire' which is 'inside you' (p.234), even when it seems unbearably difficult to do so. (The 'fire' can be interpreted as McCarthy's term for the human spirit.) Both books recognise that there is inherent value in maintaining human virtues in difficult circumstances. By surviving in harsh conditions, we demonstrate our will to retain the best aspects of humanity.

## Human triviality and weakness

**Key quote**

'... all I see is people being washed away by life ...' (p.47)

For Amsterdam, human nature is remarkably unchangeable. Although the world is often physically unrecognisable, the people who live in it are instantly familiar. The characters, even though they are living in difficult times, retain all the petty grievances, jealousies and capacity for self-delusion that we recognise in ourselves. For example:

> When I was evacuating people, they knew why I was standing in their doorway, but they'd come up with a thousand questions all of which were attempts to stall or to find some loophole in reality that would mean they would stay in their homes. It never changed the facts. (p.70)

The people forced to exist in this unpleasant future are vulnerable, flawed and aching for security. While we all might hope that humanity will 'rise to the occasion' when threatened, *Things We Didn't See Coming* suggests that people generally act in their own self-interest, and will lie to themselves when necessary as a means of self-preservation. For example, the narrator in *Dry Land* admits that 'the real reward is having the pick of abandoned property' (p.47), rather than any greater desire to do good for other people.

The most striking aspect of Amsterdam's characters is their familiarity. Although their surroundings are extremely degraded, they still act as if the appalling condition of their natural environment were not a reality. Amsterdam has argued that the novel is about 'the little things that will always be closest to our concerns: where will I be sleeping, and with whom?' (*Literary Minded* 2009). The protagonist fails to be worried about the 'right' things, preferring to worry about matters that are closer to his – and to our – heart. These are not necessarily the most noble characteristics, either – most of the time, people just want to be warm and fed, with little interest in self-sacrifice. However, Amsterdam does not condemn these simple needs; rather, he implies that it is unrealistic to expect people to act with extraordinary heroism and selflessness when they are simply trying to scratch out a basic living for themselves.

## Wastefulness and decadence

**Key quote**

'... I saw her toss a bracelet that was so heavy with pink diamonds you could hear it over the engine when it hit the floor.' (p.106)

The enduring human tendency to create waste is particularly obvious in *The Theft That Got Me Here*, when the narrator travels through 'suburbia', now a devastated and deserted buffer zone between the prison-like city and the comparatively lush countryside:

> So there's all these little mansions, all this real estate, empty and worthless – whole houses look gutted, like cars that have been stripped and put up on blocks. Grandpa says, 'Plenty ironic – these suburbanites who want life both ways out here end up losing the most'. (p.32)

The theme of a society destroyed by its own craving for decadence recurs several times, for example, in the narrator's description of the house in *Dry Land*:

> Inside, the place is all fake-rustic, with a family of black skillets hanging over the kitchen counter, patchwork quilts on the walls everywhere, and the thousand-dollar appliances you can't use since the grid went down. (p.49)

The kitchen was once splendid, but the appalling conditions of life surrounding it make its extravagance look ridiculous. In her book *Blubberland*, Elizabeth Farrelly explains how our obsession with suburban luxury is destructive:

> Gone are the days when presence was vulgar and taste, not to say courtesy, required a degree of understatement or even tact ... It's as though our childhood yearnings to play kings and queens, to wear ermine and live forever in vast palaces, still haunt us;

> as though personal opulence is still the biggest and brightest outpost of our imagining. (Farrelly 2008, p.100)

As Amsterdam's book shows, this craving for luxury is unsustainable. It all falls apart as society becomes unable to supply itself with the massive amounts of resources needed to sustain these palaces. Wealth is no protection against the harsher elements of life, as the rich and the comfortable are ultimately subject to the same limitations as the rest of us.

## Predictions of the future: technology, practices and innovations

The novel is notable for its surprising lack of emphasis on cutting-edge technology – the future world is described as quite like our own, albeit with an impoverished natural environment. Although new technologies are mentioned in almost every story, they are introduced subtly. Amsterdam does this to give the impression that technology is part of the fabric of everyday life. All the same, there are some innovations mentioned in most stories, for example:

- *The Theft That Got Me Here* features city/country ID cards and corn-based biofuels.
- *Dry Land* features 'solar sheets' (p.49), which seem similar to solar panels.
- *Uses for Vinegar* features 'pop-up barracks' (p.85).

The inconspicuous way in which technology is integrated into the novel's world is also interesting. Amsterdam consciously tried to make his vision different from the typical science fiction novel. He states sarcastically, 'We all know what the city of the future is going to look like, right? Either shiny and sleek or grimy and run by gadgets gone bad' (Meyer 2010). *Things We Didn't See Coming* avoids these extremes by setting most of the action in a heavily *rural* environment, unlike most science fiction, which almost always deals with *urban* life.

## The hostility of nature

**Key quote**

'As I was walking here, I heard about a mob driving up to one of the larger protected settlements and blinding fifteen soldiers with chemicals, just so they could take their weapons. Old-style hatred is back.' (p.142)

Charles Darwin's *On the Origin of Species*, one of the most influential books in history, was published in 1859. The book was hugely influential – but it was also intensely controversial, and many people resented Darwin's vision of nature as a system that was utterly indifferent to human and animal suffering. Prior to Darwin's time, most people had a benevolent view of the natural world, as containing 'all things bright and beautiful, all creatures great and small'.

Human technology is able to make nature far less cruel, harsh and wasteful (think again of how much we rely on sewerage systems for our health and wellbeing). But in *Things We Didn't See Coming*, nature has reasserted itself in a manner that demonstrates its utter indifference to humankind's fate. There are no lush pastures left in the end, just barren plains and scrubby vegetation. Robbed of its ecological base, humanity is locked into an animalistic struggle to survive.

## The Wanderer/The 'Man with No Name'

The main character does not stay in any one place for very long, nor does he have a name. He is a 'wandering' figure, primarily an observer, who describes the problems of his world to the reader without imposing his personality too heavily on the book.

The wandering narrator is essentially a passive, enigmatic figure. His personality is kept mysterious and relatively unobtrusive, so that we are able to observe physical events as clearly as possible. One of the protagonist's key features is his lack of roots. Exiled from his birthplace, he wanders until he eventually finds a place to stay.

## The need for love and companionship

The book reminds us of the human need to be romantically and sexually desired by another person. Even when the narrator is facing quite worrying circumstances, he is often focused on the challenges of 'getting laid'. His friendship with Margo, with whom he doesn't really get along, is driven by his clear need for another human being to love and protect him.

This impulse is clearest in *Cakewalk*, where a man on the verge of death urges the narrator to 'let me finish talking to you before you board up the door' (p.72). Clearly, his thirst for companionship overrides any consideration for others' safety. As Amsterdam himself says, 'It wasn't the floods and plagues that were his trials ... he seems to go for a very long time without love' (Jordan 2009). The narrator's overwhelming need to be near someone else overpowers his obvious physical suffering.

## Disease, sickness and bodily fragility

Bodily breakdown, dysfunction and decay are central to the novel. Amsterdam 'wanted illness, not just bird flu and the like, to have a part in this future' (Meyer 2010). People undergo many types of bodily deterioration, and are often in pain from various ailments. The virus afflicts many in the landscape, including the ill stranger in *Cakewalk*. People's hormonal makeup becomes permanently stunted. Most graphically, by the end of the novel, the population is literally falling apart from skin cancer, which reduces people to bleeding, peeling masses of flesh. Even before this, the narrator is in constant pain from his various ailments.

By exposing the reader to the full extent of bodily infirmities, *Things We Didn't See Coming* provides a serious corrective to our airbrushed ideas of human perfection.

## The breakdown of the 'social contract'

The 'social contract' refers to the agreement that people must enter into a type of 'contract' in order to exist peacefully together in a society. For a peaceful society to exist, the citizens must agree to give up some of their rights. For example, if I choose to be a law-abiding citizen, I must give up my right to steal other people's possessions. Society's law against stealing restricts my personal freedom – but it also allows other people to live in relative harmony with one another, under the protection of the law.

In *Things We Didn't See Coming*, this positive idea of a social contract as something that protects people from harm seems to be breaking down. Most obviously, because there simply isn't enough food to go around, obeying the law against stealing isn't so easy. Also, because the political institutions are so corrupt, people are no longer adequately protected by the law.

This breakdown of law and order eventually causes society to break up into smaller, self-contained groups with the power to create their own laws, as we can see in *Predisposed* and *The Profit Motive*. Overall, though, the book suggests that society requires a strong social contract in order to function properly.

## DIFFERENT INTERPRETATIONS

Different interpretations arise from different responses to a text. Over time, a text will evoke a wide range of responses from its readers, who may come from various social or cultural groups and live in very different places and historical periods. These responses may be published in newspapers, journals and books by critics and reviewers, or expressed in discussions among readers in the media, classrooms, book groups and so on. While there is no single correct reading or interpretation of a text, it is important to understand that an interpretation is more than an 'opinion' – it is the justification of a point of view on the text. To present an interpretation of the text based on your point of view you must use a logical argument and support it with relevant evidence from the text.

Most reviewers cited have complex positions on *Things We Didn't See Coming*; however, for simplicity's sake, I have tried to deal with the two main strands of argument used by critics. While this doesn't mean that there are *only two* possible readings of the text, it does suggest that the issue of morality is foremost in many critics' minds, as well as in the author's.

## Interpretation 1

***Things We Didn't See Coming* is a pessimistic story of humanity's capacity for immorality and self-delusion.**

This interpretation sees the novel as showing humanity's weakness in the face of crisis. Several critics have argued that the negative themes of Amsterdam's novel dwell on humanity's failure to deal with catastrophic situations. Literary blogger 'Madbibliophile', for example, argues:

> The ideas of our heavy reliance on industrialisation and unsustainable mass consumption, health care, heavy medication of the human body and climate and environmental change are some of the issues that [underlie] the stories. (Madbibliophile 2010)

Lisa McLendon of *The Wichita Eagle* also comments on the novel's pessimistic opinion of humanity:

> Most of the people in *Things We Didn't See Coming*, a sharp debut from Steven Amsterdam, not only didn't see things coming, they refuse to see them once they're here. (McLendon 2010)

Catherine Ford agrees, noting that in Amsterdam's novel, 'the human race has stumbled even further down the path of self-annihilation' (Ford 2009).

The many examples of indefensible human behaviour described by Amsterdam in the book certainly seem to support this reading. On his journey, the protagonist is surrounded by some of the worst examples of flawed humanity. Sometimes, this type of behaviour seems understandable – for example, the mother's attempt on the narrator's life in *Dry Land* could be interpreted as an example of the protective instinct. Even though it is extreme, it is still based on something real.

Yet the behaviour of Margo and Juliet is less understandable. They seem to be purely concerned with hedonism (pleasure-seeking) and destruction. If the book is to be interpreted at all optimistically, these examples present very real difficulties. It is possible that they are uniquely bad people in a moral world; however, it is more likely that there are many more people just like them.

Perhaps the most logical way to look at the world of *Things We Didn't See Coming* is as an environment in which it is impossible to be fully good. If this perspective is taken, then the narrator's disgust with stealing is simply not logical. People must do what they can to survive, and morality hinders this ability. Old-fashioned morality, then, may be seen as a luxury that most people in the novel simply cannot afford. Survival always comes first, morality always comes a distant second. Given this truth, the self-delusion and immorality of many of the characters may simply be logical responses to their desperately impoverished situation.

## Interpretation 2

**Despite its apparent pessimism, *Things We Didn't See Coming* is in fact a life-affirming book.**

This interpretation sees a core of humanity at the book's heart. Although many characters in the stories are broken and damaged by their fate, more often than not they attempt to assist each other when they can – even if this puts them at risk.

The majority of critics see the novel as a more upbeat interpretation of humanity's ability to cope with whatever is thrown at it. Taylor Antrim of *The Daily Beast* writes, 'The future's a mess. Amsterdam's book says get used to it, roll with the punches, do your best' (Antrim 2010). *Reading Matters* blog agrees that the novel 'has the potential to be a cold, brutal and violent book, but instead it's a heady mix of tenderness, sexiness, hopefulness and wonder' (*Reading Matters* 2010). Similarly, Carl Hays of *Booklist* claims that 'the disasters' exact causes are kept vague and mercifully free of authorial finger-pointing at humanity's presumable role in creating them' (Hays 2010).

Finally, *The Australian* argues that the book supports the view that 'there is good to be found in almost all abysmal situations', while the *Brisbane Courier-Mail* critic makes the joke that 'It's the end of the world as we know it, but there is always hope' (Ross 2009).

These 'upbeat' interpretations claim that the bad things that happen are outweighed by the positives. Overall, this interpretation sees the book as an uplifting study of the triumph of human strength over adversity. If we are able to get past the apparent heartlessness of this world, there is much to admire in the behaviour of ordinary people. The father's example is instructive. While he does seem to be acting in an extreme and erratic manner in the first story, his behaviour is eventually vindicated by later events.

Even the people in the narrator's family who *don't* fully understand what's happening are only acting as best they can to ensure that the family stays together. The grandparents, while ill-suited to the world in which they live, are obviously affectionate to the narrator. Similarly, Cate, the narrator's mother, tries her best to prevent her husband from breaking up their family.

Later in the book, there are significant positive examples of human relationships and behaviour among the negative ones. The most prominent of these, of course, is the father-son type relationship formed between the narrator and Jeph. Their love for each other is not fully expressed but it is strongly implied. In his own way, Jeph does everything he can to help the narrator back to health; similarly, the narrator seems to do all in his power to ensure that Jeph receives a relatively normal and healthy upbringing. Although he eventually abandons the village, this is not because he lacks affection for Jeph.

Virtually everyone in the novel is under extreme stress. When people feel that their options are severely limited, they can't always behave in ways that we would necessarily find acceptable. Imagine how you would behave in such a horrible situation – it quite possibly wouldn't be in ways commonly considered 'nice' or 'normal'. In this sense, the characters can be viewed in a positive light on the whole: it is their *circumstances* that are virtually unbearable. With these flawed yet mostly decent characters, the author is making the point that to think that people will behave in exactly the same ways under all situations is unrealistic.

Although Amsterdam has written a work that cannot be summed up easily, there are some broad themes on which most reviewers agree. Critics on each side of the argument, whether they have a positive or negative perspective about the book, seem to agree that the author is mainly concerned about *human behaviour*. The issues exposed by the book's extraordinary events are relevant across all genres. The protagonist's struggle to gain Margo's love and acceptance is familiar from many other works of fiction, as is his conflict with his father. Despite their many differences, critics almost unanimously agree that *Things We Didn't See Coming* offers a complex, dark and revealing picture of human nature.

# QUESTIONS & ANSWERS

This section focuses on your own analytical writing on the text, and gives you strategies for producing highquality responses in your coursework and exam essays.

## Essay writing: an overview

An essay is a formal and serious piece of writing that presents your point of view on the text, usually in response to a given essay topic. Your 'point of view' in an essay is your interpretation of the meaning of the text's language, structure, characters, situations and events, supported by detailed analysis of textual evidence.

### Analyse – don't summarise

In your essay it is important to avoid simply summarising what happens in a text:

- A **summary** is a description or paraphrase (retelling in different words) of the characters and events, e.g. 'Macbeth has a horrifying vision of a dagger dripping with blood before he goes to murder King Duncan'
- An **analysis** is an explanation of the real meaning or significance that lies 'beneath' the text's words (and images, for a film). For example: 'Macbeth's vision of a bloody dagger shows how deeply uneasy he is about the violent act he is contemplating – as well as his sense that supernatural forces are impelling him to act'.

A limited amount of summary is sometimes necessary to let your reader know which part of the text you wish to discuss. However, always keep this to a minimum and follow it immediately with your analysis (explanation) of what this part of the text is really telling us.

### Plan your essay

Carefully plan your essay so that you have a clear idea of what you are going to say. The plan ensures that your ideas flow logically, that your argument remains consistent and that you stay on the topic. An essay plan should be a list of **brief dot points** – no more than half a page. It includes:

- your central argument or main contention – a concise statement (usually in a single sentence) of your overall response to the topic. See 'Analysing a sample topic' for guidelines on how to formulate a main contention.
- three or four dot points for each paragraph indicating the main idea and evidence/examples from the text. Note that in your essay you will need to *expand* on these points and *analyse* the evidence.

### Structure your essay

An essay is a complete, self-contained piece of writing. It has a clear beginning (the introduction), middle (several body paragraphs) and end (the last paragraph or conclusion). It must also have a central argument that runs throughout, linking each paragraph to form a coherent whole.

See examples of introductions and conclusions in the 'Analysing a sample topic' and 'Sample answer' sections.

**The introduction establishes your overall response to the topic**. It includes your main contention and outlines the main evidence you will refer to in the course of the essay. Write your introduction *after* you have done a plan and *before* you write the rest of the essay.

**The body paragraphs argue your case** – they present evidence from the text and explain how this evidence supports your argument. Each body paragraph needs:

- a strong **topic sentence** (usually the first sentence) that states the main point being made in the paragraph
- **evidence** from the text, including some brief quotations
- **analysis** of the textual evidence explaining its significance and **explanation** of how it supports your argument
- **links back to the topic** in one or more statements, usually towards the end of the paragraph.

Connect the body paragraphs so that your discussion flows smoothly. Use some linking words and phrases such as 'similarly' and 'on the other hand', but don't start every paragraph like this. Another strategy is to use a significant word from the last sentence of one paragraph in the first sentence of the next.

Use key terms from the topic – or synonyms for them – throughout, so the relevance of your discussion to the topic is always clear.

**The conclusion ties everything together and finishes the essay.** It includes strong statements that emphasise your central argument and provide a clear response to the topic.

Avoid simply restating the points made earlier in the essay – this will end on a very flat note and imply that you have run out of ideas and vocabulary. The conclusion is meant to be a logical extension of what you have written, rather than a repetition or summary of it. Writing an effective conclusion can be a challenge. Some tips follow.

- Start by linking back to the final sentence of the second-last paragraph – this helps your writing to 'flow', rather than just leaping back to your main contention straight away.
- Use synonyms and expressions with equivalent meanings to vary your vocabulary. This allows you to reinforce your line of argument without being repetitive.
- When planning your essay, think of one or two broad statements or observations about the text's wider meaning. These should be related to the topic and your overall argument. Keep them for the conclusion, since they will give you something 'new' to say but still follow logically from your discussion. The introduction will be focused on the topic, but the conclusion can present a wider view of the text.

## Vocabulary for writing on the text

***Apocalyptic:*** concerning the end of the world. The word comes from the final book of the New Testament, which depicts the end of the world and the return of Jesus Christ. Much of *Things We Didn't See Coming* can be viewed as taking place in an apocalyptic environment.

***Black humour:*** a type of humour based on things that we would normally consider morbid or depressing.

***Chronological structure:*** the order in which events are organised in the novel. The chronological structure of *Things We Didn't See Coming* contains several flashbacks.

**Decadence:** the state of desiring or consuming far more than is necessary. In some ways, *Things We Didn't See Coming* comments on the destructive effects of decadence on our society.

**Dystopian/Utopian:** a 'utopia' is a world where everything is perfect, whereas a 'dsytopia' is a world in which everything is unpleasant. *Things We Didn't See Coming* can be interpreted as a 'dystopian' novel.

**Irony:** a tone that draws attention to the difference between how something *actually is* and how something *should be*. The narrator's voice is sometimes ironic: he uses a jokey, casual tone, even when circumstances are difficult or dangerous. Talking of Juliet, for example, the narrator says: 'The last time she planned a treat for us, we went to her island and were administered a fungus while listening to some healer of the moment' (p.103). Here, the narrator is using an ironic tone to tell us that Juliet is a superficial and decadent person.

**Science fiction:** a genre set in the future, largely concerned with how humans use technology.

**Social contract:** the political idea that people will give up some of their freedom in exchange for an increased sense of security when they become members of society. In *Things We Didn't See Coming*, the 'social contract' is gradually being replaced by violence and disorder.

## Essay topics

1. '*Things We Didn't See Coming* demonstrates that people of honesty and integrity will triumph in the end.' Discuss.
2. 'There are no bad characters in *Things We Didn't See Coming*. Everyone is just doing the best they can to survive.' Do you agree?
3. 'The text shows a society in which facts are uncertain, relationships are temporary and decisions are based purely on self-interest.' How does the narrative of *Things We Didn't See Coming* convey this view of a future society?
4. "Now is as good a time as any to change", says the narrator. Are the characters in the novel capable of change?
5. '*Things We Didn't See Coming* strongly suggests that humankind deserves its suffering.' Do you agree?

6 How does the physical environment influence the characters' behaviour in *Things We Didn't See Coming*?

7 '*Things We Didn't See Coming* is completely devoid of hope.' Do you agree?

8 'Amsterdam's novel is life-affirming, because it shows how love can provide solace in times of need.' Discuss.

9 'Although the protagonist is not a traditional heroic figure, his struggle against the temptation of stealing ultimately makes him a hero.' Do you agree?

10 '*Things We Didn't See Coming* can be interpreted as a scathing criticism of our present-day society.' Discuss.

## Analysing a sample topic

**'*Things We Didn't See Coming* is completely devoid of hope.' Do you agree?**

This question asks you to analyse the text's outlook. To do this, you will have to decide whether there is any presence of hope in the narrative. It's important to determine what *kind* of hope is being referred to. For example, it is clear that the novel is not hopeful about environmental issues, as the future environment is unambiguously oppressive.

### Consider the evidence

Considering the character of the protagonist is a logical place to start. Because we view the world of the novel through his eyes, we directly experience his viewpoint. As we don't have access to other characters' thoughts, we can only interpret their actions via the protagonist. It is therefore often very difficult to gauge whether they are fundamentally hopeful or not. Other characters' minds are largely mysterious to us, and we have to interpret their thoughts indirectly.

Begin by looking at the collection's first story, when the protagonist is a young boy of 10. Although his father paints an extremely negative picture of the future, claiming that everything is about to 'fall apart'(p.13), his tenacious love for his son suggests that he is still capable of optimism, however muted. Even though the father holds no hope that the environment will remain inhabitable, he still clearly believes in the power of love.

If we move forward in time to the following stories, we notice that there is not much in the way of *explicit* hope. Things deteriorate very quickly – for example, the protagonist's grandfather killing himself and his wife can be read as a symbol of the old world's despair. In the new, cynical reality, people behave as if this is their last day on Earth, thinking only of their own wishes. The trio's ill-fated journey out of the city, and towards the elusive paradise of Bell's Brook, can be seen as a new low point, as there is no longer any pretence that things will turn out for the best. The grandparents' deaths, then, seem to sacrifice any sense of hope associated with our own world.

Given the above points, you could make a perfectly reasonable argument in agreement with the contention that the novel is too depressing to leave room for hope. In environmental terms, there is never any sign that things are *ever* going to get any better: they consistently get worse until the world we know is scarcely recognisable. It has been replaced by a kind of Hell, seemingly unfit for human habitation. By the time of *Uses for Vinegar*, in which people are being herded into squalid refugee camps, all hope seems to have evaporated. These points can be used in support of the contention.

The occupations held by the protagonist offer further evidence of the novel's lack of hope. After his adolescence, the protagonist becomes engaged in a series of dangerous, uncomfortable and underappreciated jobs that are mostly focused on evacuating people in need from hazardous locations. They also require him to take a distinctly hard-line position in regard to other people's wishes. Clearly, circumstances have forced him to give up the gentleness and sensitivity that characterised him in the first story. You could use several examples from the text to support this point.

However, it would also be a good idea to deal with the other side of the argument as well. Rather than agreeing with the contention, perhaps it would be beneficial to look for *alternative* avenues for hope. This will give your essay a more complex narrative tone, and will therefore demonstrate that you have thought in detail about the issue's complex implications.

What, then, would be alternative ground for hope in the novel? A productive direction to take might be the presence of *internal* hope in the narrative – that is, the presence of faith in the narrator and others. While the external situation continues to deteriorate, there is considerable evidence that this more internal sense of hope persists. Evidence that you could use to illustrate this alternative viewpoint includes:

- the protagonist's efforts to help other people (e.g. Jenna), even at considerable cost to himself
- his obvious need for love, including his ongoing involvement with, and protection of, Margo
- his temporary, but sincere, taking on of the role of Jeph's guardian
- his constant struggle with the morality of stealing, and his eventual refusal to do this in the penultimate story, along with the revelation that he is 'too old for theft' (p.154)
- his reconciliation with his father in *Best Medicine*.

Due to the clear lack of hope that the environment will ever be restored to its original glory, this internal narrative of hope offers an alternative to the external narrative of hopelessness. By dealing with the two strands of the argument in this way, your essay will gain the complex focus required.

### Sample introduction

By most standards, *Things We Didn't See Coming* is clearly not an uplifting book. It deals with an unfolding environmental catastrophe that displaces, or throws into extreme hardship, the majority of the population. The wretched conditions that many people are forced to endure are harrowing, as is the emotional hardness caused by chronic resource shortages and declining living conditions. Yet the novel is not entirely without hope, which comes from a quite unlikely source: the nameless protagonist. The protagonist, who does not seem to be made of heroic material, undergoes an internal struggle against vice that proves his capacity for transcending his unpromising circumstances. His protracted moral struggles throughout the narrative are sufficient to offer the reader a glimpse of something better. Trapped within a blighted world, he never stops hoping, loving, and dreaming. In the end, despite the wretched conditions, he manages to offer a sense of hope.

# SAMPLE ANSWER

**'*Things We Didn't See Coming* suggests that humankind deserves its suffering.' Do you agree?**

The apocalyptic environmental collapses depicted in *Things We Didn't See Coming* are characterised as a type of vengeance for the human race's moral vanity and self-centredness. Over and over, the characters show an appalling lack of judgement and an inability to process what is happening in the wider world. In times of extreme stress, when they would do best to respond collectively to what is going on around them, the characters respond instead by retreating into selfish actions. However, this is far from the whole story. In fact, the author's significant faith in humanity suggests that these people are being assaulted by forces that they did very little, if anything, to deserve. This ambivalent picture of humankind's culpability, of people's refusal to explicitly condemn or condone the behaviour that led up to the crisis, is one of the book's major strengths. Ultimately, it is not possible to form a definitive judgement either way about the author's attitude toward humankind's guilt.

Many characters in the book behave in counterproductive ways. The clearest representatives of this attitude are the protagonist's grandparents, who are characterised by an inability to process the gravity of their situation. Their responses to crises are trivial and self-centred. It is probably significant that they are part of the 'baby boomer' generation (they 'honeymooned back in the sixties, the old hippies'), which enjoyed unprecedented levels of material wealth yet has done little to address the grave environmental crises we are currently facing. But they are still painted as helpless victims of the situation; they are far too sympathetic as characters to fully 'deserve' what is happening to them. Despite their flaws, they are portrayed as ignorant rather than malicious figures.

The similarities between the environmental catastrophes and biblical plagues provide stronger evidence of humanity's guilt. The protagonist describes himself as 'fallen', a term that explicitly refers to Adam and Eve's state after being exiled from Eden, and strongly implies that he's to blame for his own misfortunes. The father, in the first chapter, seems to share this pessimistic view of humankind. He tells his son that the blame for coming events can be laid at humanity's feet:

> This whole thing is symbolic, symbolic of a system that's hopelessly short-sighted, a system that twenty, thirty years ago couldn't imagine a time when we might be starting a new century. That's how limited an animal we are.

This quote definitely suggests that humans are mostly flawed beings, incapable of acting for the greater good. If the father's interpretation is taken at face value, it is very difficult to sympathise with the plight of humanity in subsequent stories.

The idea of being 'fallen' also lends support to the idea that humanity is to blame for the problems that confront it. The protagonist returns to this theme throughout, while the father provides the most explicit evidence of humankind's culpability:

> We are arrogant, stupid – we lack humility in the face of centuries and centuries of time before us ... What we know now is that we didn't think enough. We didn't worry about the right things.

The 'we' in the father's dialogue here is, clearly, humanity itself. His judgement seems unfair at the time, yet it is vindicated in subsequent chapters. By ignoring the future consequences of its selfish actions, humanity has condemned itself to a miserable future.

The debris of human decadence that litters the landscape is further evidence of the idea of retribution for humanity's sins. There is no sign anywhere that humanity has learned to moderate its appetites in the face of necessity; instead, it seems that everyone has chosen to steer society off a cliff rather than preserve it. The protagonist frequently comes across expensive luxury objects that have been rendered useless in the collapsed environment, suggesting that our relentless 'greed is good' mentality has played a large part in destroying our lives.

On the other hand, much of *Things We Didn't See Coming* suggests that humanity *is* capable of redeeming itself. The rapid change of the community structure depicted forces people to act in a more co-operative way, with the result that a more communal sense of obligation is arrived at. The system of government implemented in *The Profit Motive*, for example, while elitist, is intended to offer an alternative to the self-centred system of acting purely for immediate personal gain.

Judging by the ways in which characters act throughout the novel, humanity is not blameless in the crisis. People are selfish; they do not act for the common good; their actions are environmentally destructive. The character of Margo, in particular, can be seen as a representative of this kind of human weakness. On the other hand, the author's decision to narrate the novel from the perspective of a character who obviously has difficulty conquering his own personal weaknesses makes the extent of humanity's impact on the environment far more understandable. While *Things We Didn't See Coming* does not flinch from exposing humanity's flawed nature, it does not entirely blame the victims for the crisis through which they are forced to live.

# REFERENCES & READING


Amsterdam, Steven 2009, *Things We Didn't See Coming,* Sleepers, Collingwood.

Antrim, Taylor 2010, 'A Great Dystopian Novel', *The Daily Beast,* 30 March 2010, http://www.thedailybeast.com/blogs-and-stories/2010-03-30/a-great-dystopian-novel/, accessed 10 June 2010.

Armanno, Venero 2009, 'Light Edge on a Dark Road', *The Australian,* 4 April 2009, http://www.stevenamsterdam.com/TWDSC_Australian_Reviews.html, accessed 11 July 2010.

*The Bible: King James Version* (2001), Oxford World's Classics, Oxford.

Brooks, David 2010, 'The Culture of Exposure', *New York Times,* 25 June 2010, http://www.nytimes.com/2010/06/25/opinion/25brooks.html?ref=davidbrooks, accessed 1 July 2010.

Cuarón, Alfonso 2006, *Children of Men*, Universal Pictures.

Cunningham, Sophie 2010, 'Sophie Cunningham Talks to Steven Amsterdam', *Meanjin,* http://meanjin.com.au/spike-the-meanjin-blog/post/new-territories-sophie-cunningham-talks-to-steven-amsterdam/, accessed 14 June 2010.

Defoe, Daniel 2009 [1719], *Robinson Crusoe*, Oxford World's Classics, Oxford.

Diamond, Jared 2005, *Collapse*, Penguin, London.

Drummond, Katie 2010, 'Darpa: US Geek Shortage is National Security Risk', *Wired*, 15 January 2010, http://www.wired.com/dangerroom/2010/01/darpa-us-geek-shortage-is-a-national-security-risk, accessed 24 July 2010.

Farrelly, Elizabeth 2008, *Blubberland: The Dangers of Happiness,* The MIT Press, Cambridge.

Ford, Catherine 2009, 'Review of *Things We Didn't See* Coming', in *Australian Literary Review*, Volume 4, Issue 2 (March 2009), http://www.stevenamsterdam.com/TWDSC_Australian_Reviews.html, accessed 11 July 2010.

Golding, William 1999, *Lord of the Flies*, Faber, London.

Goodman, Geoffrey 1995, 'Obituary: Harold Wilson', *The Guardian,* 25 May 1995, http://www.guardian.co.uk/politics/1995/may/25/obituaries, accessed 14 July 2010.

Hamilton, Clive 2010, *Requiem for a Species: Why We Resist the Truth about Climate Change*, Allen & Unwin, Crow's Nest.

Harris, Paul and Townsend, Mark 2004, 'Now the Pentagon Tells Bush: Climate Change Will Destroy Us', *The Guardian*, 22 February 2004, http://www.guardian.co.uk/environment/2004/feb/22/usnews.theobserver, accessed 15 July 2010.

Hays, Carl 2010, 'Review of *Things We Didn't See Coming*', *Booklist*, 1 February 2010, http://www.stevenamsterdam.com/TWDSC_American_Reviews.html, accessed 17 September 2010.

Herbert, Bob, 'Following BP's Lead', *New York Times*, 24 May 2009, http://www.nytimes.com/2010/05/25/opinion/25herbert.html, accessed 15 July 2010.

Hobbes, Thomas 2004 [1651] Leviathan, http://www.gutenberg.org/files/3207/3207.txt, accessed 15 July 2010.

Holland, Tom 2009, *Millennium*, Abacus, London.

Hutchinson, Tracee 2007, 'Time to Remember the Tampa Debacle', in *The Age*, 25 August 2007, http://www.theage.com.au/news/opinion/time-to-remember-the-tampa-debacle/2007/08/24/1187462515471.html, accessed 24 July 2010.

Jordan, Toni 2009, 'Profile of Steven Amsterdam', in *The Big Issue*, 6 March 2009, http://www.stevenamsterdam.com/Profile_of_Steven_Amsterdam_by_Toni_Jordan.html, accessed 18 July 2010.

Kamiya, Gary 2007, 'Review of 'Are We Rome?', in *Salon*, 7 June 2007, http://www.salon.com/books/review/2007/06/07/rome, accessed 15 July 2010.

*Literary Minded Blog*, 2009, http://bookworm-megs.blogspot.com/2009/06/author-interview-steven-amsterdam.html, accessed 12 July 2010.

McCarthy, Cormac 2006, *The Road*, Alfred A Knopf, New York.

McLendon, Lisa 2010, 'Book Takes an Alternate View of the Future', The Wichita Eagle, 14 February 2010, http://www.stevenamsterdam.com/TWDSC_American_Reviews.html, accessed 11 July 2010.

Meyer, Angela 2010, 'Steven Amsterdam: A Responsive Interview', *Crikey*, http://blogs.crikey.com.au/literaryminded/2009/03/23/steven-amsterdam-a-responsive-interview/, accessed 14 June 2010.

Milton, John 2004 [1667], *Paradise Lost*, W. W. Norton & Co., New York.

Rabelais, Kevin 2009, 'Interview with Steven Amsterdam', *Readings Australian Feature Series*, 4 March 2009.

'Review of *Things We Didn't See Coming*', in *Mad Bibliophile*, July 2010, http://madbibliophile.wordpress.com/2010/02/07/review-things-we-didnt-see-coming-by-steve-amsterdam, accessed 11 July 2010.

'Review of *Things We Didn't See Coming*', in *Reading Matters*, January 2010, http://www.stevenamsterdam.com/TWDSC_UK_Reviews.html, accessed 11 July 2010.

Ross, Julia 2009, 'Steven Amsterdam's Dystopia Makes an Impressive Debut', in *Brisbane Courier-Mail*, http://www.stevenamsterdam.com/TWDSC_Australian_Reviews.html, accessed 11 July 2010.

Turner, Graham 2008, *A Comparison of Limits to Growth with Thirty Years of Reality: Socio-Economics and The Environment in Discussion, CSIRO Working Paper Series*, June 2008, http://www.csiro.au/files/files/plje.pdf, accessed 17 September 2010.